For Reference

Not to be taken from this room

AMERICAN CITIES CHRONOLOGY SERIES

ST. LOUIS
A CHRONOLOGICAL & DOCUMENTARY HISTORY

1762-1970

Compiled and Edited by
ROBERT I. VEXLER

Series Editor
HOWARD B. FURER

1974
OCEANA PUBLICATIONS, INC.
Dobbs Ferry, New York

Ref
F
474
.S2
V49

Library of Congress Cataloging in Publication Data

Vexler, Robert I
    St. Louis: a chronological and documentary history, 1762-1970.

    (American cities chronology series)
    SUMMARY: Includes a chronology of events in St. Louis' history and a selection of pertinent documents.
    Bibliography: p.
    1. St. Louis -- History -- Chronology. 2. St. Louis -- History -- Sources. [1. St. Louis -- History] I. Title.
F474.S2V49   977.8'66   74-5179
ISBN 0-379-00607-3

© Copyright 1974 by Oceana Publications, Inc.

All rights reserved. No part of this publication may be reproduced or transmitted in any form or by any means, electronic or mechanical, including photocopy, recording, xerography, or any information storage and retrieval system, without permission in writing from the publisher.

Manufactured in the United States of America.

TABLE OF CONTENTS

EDITOR'S FOREWORD. v

CHRONOLOGY 1
   Establishment and Incorporation of St. Louis, 1762-1821 1
   St. Louis as a City, 1822-1865 4
   Post-Civil War St. Louis, 1866-1876. 23
   St. Louis -- Separate from the County, 1877-1914 32
   St. Louis and Reform, 1915-1945 54
   Post-War Era and Urban Reconstruction, 1946-1970 60

DOCUMENTS 69
   First Charter of St. Louis, November 9, 1809 70
   St. Louis in 1810. 71
   First City Charter, December 9, 1822. 74
   New City Charter, 1843 78
   Creation of a Sewage System, March 12, 1849. 82
   Extension of City Limits -- Charter of 1870 83
   The Future Great City of the World, 1875 85
   Revised City Charter, July 3, 1876 88
   Scheme for Separation of the Governments of the City and
      County of St. Louis, October 22, 1876 92
   The Civic League of St. Louis, 1909. 95
   New City Charter, June 30, 1914. 97
   Segregation Ordinance, March 3, 1916 102
   Post-World War I Planning, 1918. 104
   Central River Front Plan, 1928 108
   Plans for St. Louis After World War II, December 1942. . . . 110
   Plan for Public Recreation Areas, 1944. 113
   Comprehensive City Plan, 1947 115
   St. Louis, 1951 118
   Report of Mayor's Transit Ownership Committee, 1952 121
   Housing Report, August 1953 125
   Rebuilding Industry - Commerce in St. Louis, 1953 129
   Downtown Renewal Plan, 1960. 131
   St. Louis -- Present and Future, May 7, 1961. 136

BIBLIOGRAPHY 139
   Primary Sources 139
   Secondary Sources. 144
   Articles 149

NAME INDEX. 151

EDITOR'S FOREWORD

Every effort has been made to cite the most accurate dates in the chronology; various newspapers, documents, and letters and chronicles have been consulted to determine the exact date. Later scholarship has been used to verify this information or to change dates when proven plausible.

Because the very nature of preparing a chronology of this type precludes the author from using the standard form of historical footnoting, I should like to acknowledge in this editor's foreword the major sources used to compile the bulk of the chronological and factual materials comprising the chronological section of this work: William Hyde and H. L. Conrad, eds., Encyclopedia of the History of St. Louis; McCune Gill, The St. Louis Story, 3 vols.; Ernest Kirschten, Catfish and Crystal; Isaac H. Lionberger, The Annals of St. Louis and A Brief Account of Its Foundation and Progress, 1764-1928; and Richard C. Wade, The Urban Frontier.

This research tool is compiled primarily for the student. The importance of political, social, economic and cultural events have been evaluated in relation to their significance for the development of St. Louis as one of the major cities that have contributed to the growth of America. St. Louis has played a major role in the development of the United States. Its citizens were quick to recognize the fine central location of the city on the Mississippi River and the role it could play in the industrial and commercial development of the country. St. Louis was also one of the pioneers in urban planning and has made use of the valuable knowledge accrued immediately before and after the Second World War to redevelop her downtown area as well as to encourage the reconstruction of industry and commerce in order to improve the role of St. Louis in relation to the development of the nation as a whole.

Documents have been selected which best illustrate the major aspects in the development of St. Louis from the small early American town to the bustling and growing city of the 1960's.

Robert I. Vexler
Briarcliff College

ESTABLISHMENT AND INCORPORATION OF ST. LOUIS, 1762-1821

1762	November. Louis XV of France gave Louisiana to the King of Spain on paper, but it was kept an international secret.
1763	December. Pierre Laclede Liguest, working partner of Maxent, Laclede and Company of New Orleans, chose the site of St. Louis. He had started up the Mississippi River in August.
1764	February 14. Pierre Laclede sent his young lieutenant Auguste Chouteau up the Mississippi River to begin the settlement of St. Louis.
	April. Laclede came to the site of the settlement, naming it St. Louis in honor of Louis XV and of the King's patron, Saint Louis IX.
1767	The first horse racing was held on the prairie adjoining the St. Louis settlement.
1770	June 24. The first Catholic church in St. Louis was dedicated.
1774	Jean Baptiste Trudeau established a school for boys.
	St. Louis was established as a village.
1779	The Indians attacked women and children picking berries outside of the town and killed many of them.
1780	General George Rogers Clark established Fort Jefferson on the eastern bank of the Mississippi a little below the mouth of the Ohio River.
	May 26. The Indians attacked St. Louis. It was attributed to British influence, but it was probably the result of incitement by guerillas for plunder.
1781	January 2. Captain Beausoliel and sixty-five residents of St. Louis as well as their Indian allies left St. Louis to make a return "coup" for the attack in 1780. They attacked the British port of St. Joseph.
1794	The Missouri Trading Company was organized by all the traders of St. Louis as a cooperative trading company.

1797	Captain James Piggott began running a ferry from St. Louis across the Mississippi to Illinois.
	Madame Marie Payant Rigauche opened a school.
1800	October 1. The Treaty of Ildefonso provided for the Spaniards to return the Territory of Louisiana to France.
1802	July 12. The first newspaper, <u>The Missouri Gazette</u>, appeared. Its name was later changed to <u>The Missouri Republican</u>.
1803	April 30. The Louisiana Purchase was completed by the United States.
1804	The first English school was established by Mr. Rotchford.
	Governor William Henry Harrison negotiated the Treaty of St. Louis with the chiefs of the united nations of the Sacs and Foxes for their claim to the immense tract of country lying between the Illinois and Mississippi Rivers.
	December 18. The first term of the County Court was held.
1805	August 9. Zebulon M. Pike set out from St. Louis on his first expedition to trace the Mississippi to its source. He returned nine months later.
	September. Aaron Burr came to St. Louis a few months after he retired from the vice-presidency. He found no encouragement for his southwestern empire.
1806	Zebulon M. Pike left St. Louis to explore the Louisiana Territory. He penetrated the Rocky Mountain region and discovered Pike's Peak.
1807	Captain Merriwether Lewis was appointed governor of the territory by President Jefferson. He served until his death in 1809.
1808	September 15. St. Louis Lodge No. 3 of the Masons was chartered by the Grand Lodge of Pennsylvania.
1809	Benjamin Howard was appointed governor of the territory by President Madison. He served until 1813 when he resigned.

CHRONOLOGY

	November 9. St. Louis Town was incorporated by the territorial legislature.
1812	Dakota Park was given to the town.
	A mail route was established between St. Louis and Shawneetown.
	The first public market was established.
1813	Captain William Clark was appointed territorial governor of Missouri. He remained in office until the state of Missouri entered the Union in 1820.
1815	The Western Journal was first published. Its name was changed to The Emigrant in 1816 and to The Enquirer shortly thereafter. Its name was finally changed to The Beacon in 1827, and it was discontinued in 1832.
1816	The Bank of St. Louis was opened.
	Fort Armstrong was built on Rock Island.
1817	The Bank of Missouri was established.
	The first steamboat, the Pike, arrived at St. Louis.
	Construction of the Missouri Hotel was begun. It was completed in 1819.
	The first courthouse was built in St. Louis.
	November. The Planters' House hotel was opened.
	November 23. Salmon Giddings organized the First Presbyterian Church in St. Louis.
1818	St. Louis Cathedral was built.
	February 9. The Irish Immigrant and Corresponding Society was formed.
	February 18. The First Baptist Church of St. Louis was organized.
	December 15. The Bible Society was founded.

1819	The state legislature passed an act granting the Wriggins Ferry Company the right to establish a ferry upon the Mississippi.
	Bishop Dubourg established a college attached to the cathedral in St. Louis. It was discontinued in 1826 and revived in 1828.
	January 27. The New Theater was opened.
	September. Rev. John Ward came to St. Louis and held his first Episcopal service on October 24.
1820	Missouri was carved out of the Missouri Territory.
	Alexander McNair was elected the governor or Missouri.
	May 20. The North Fire Company, volunteer, was organized.
	June 20. The first constitutional convention of Missouri met in St. Louis until July 19.
	August. The South Fire Company was organized.
1821	January. Jesse Walker organized a Methodist Society.

ST. LOUIS AS A CITY, 1822-1865

1822	December 9. St. Louis was incorporated as a city.
1823	March. The citizens adopted the first charter of the City of St. Louis.
	April 7. The first municipal election was held under the city charter. Dr. William Carr Lane was chosen mayor.
1824	A meeting was held in Mayor Lane's office to establish a circulating library.
	The Female Charitable Society was formed.
	March 29. An ordinance was passed to construct a wharf.
	December 24. The Missouri Advocate first appeared in St. Charles. It was moved to St. Louis on February 24, 1825.

	Its name was changed to The St. Louis Enquirer on December 24, 1826, and publication was finally suspended in 1827.
1825	The County Court appropriated $7,000 for the construction of a courthouse. It was completed in 1833.
	March. A public meeting was held in the Methodist church to form an auxiliary to the American Colonization Society in St. Louis.
1826	May. The Phoenix Fire Company was formed.
1827	John Mullanphy donated money for the establishment of the Mullanphy Orphan Asylum attached to the convent and academy of the Order of the Sacred Heart.
	St. Louis was established as a Catholic see, and the Right Reverend Joseph Rosati was appointed its first bishop by Pope Leo XII.
1828	The Mullanphy Hospital was founded.
	St. Louis University was revived and was opened in 1829. It was chartered by the Missouri Legislature in 1832.
	October 9. The Jockey Club began its races.
	November. St. Mary's Female Orphan Asylum, run by the Sisters of Charity, was established.
1829	St. Louis contracted with Messrs. John C. Wilson and Abraham Fox to build and operate a water works.
	The National Hotel was established.
	The St. Louis Times first appeared. It was published until 1832.
	A branch of the United States Bank was established with Colonel John O'Fallon as president. It wound up its affairs in 1832 when President Jackson vetoed renewal of the charter for the entire bank.
	April. Daniel O. Page was elected mayor.
1830	The population of St. Louis was 4,977.
	Construction of a new Catholic cathedral was begun.

ST. LOUIS

The first reservoir and pipes for the water system were installed.

The first type of street railway was begun.

The Argus was first published. It became known as the Union and was absorbed by the Missouri Democrat in 1852.

The Missouri Insurance Company, the first insurance company in St. Louis, was organized.

William Miller founded the sect of the Adventists.

St. Louis was made a port of entry.

1832   The Northern Fire Company, Union Company No. 2, was formed.

The first religious periodical published in St. Louis was the Catholic journal, Shepherd of the Valley.

1833   The state legislature granted a new charter to St. Louis.

The Protestant Orphan Asylum was established.

January 6. The Second Baptist Church of St. Louis was established.

April. Colonel John W. Johnston was elected mayor.

1834   The Travelers' Rest Lodge No. 1 of the Independent Order of Odd Fellows was organized in St. Louis.

The St. Louis Herald, the first daily, was issued.

The House of Refuge was established as a city institution for the detention and training of boys and girls.

November. Unitarian services were begun under the leadership of Rev. W. G. Eliot.

1835   April. John F. Darby was elected mayor.

October 31. The first number of the Anzeiger des Westens appeared as a weekly paper. It was the first German newspaper. On June 1, 1898 the paper was merged with the Westliche Post.

CHRONOLOGY

1836   Kemper College was incorporated with a university charter under the auspices of the Protestant Episcopal Church.

St. Marcus Church, the oldest German church in the city, was organized.

The Merchants' Exchange was established.

The St. Louis Medical Society was founded.

April. John F. Darby was elected mayor.

July. St. Joseph's Boys Orphan Asylum was opened under the charge of the Sisters of St. Joseph.

1837   The St. Louis Gas Light Company was incorporated with authority to establish works for manufacturing gas for lighting purposes.

The Saturday News first appeared. The Western Mirror and Ladies' Literary Gazette also were published.

The Missouri Life Insurance and Trust Company was chartered.

January 25. The St. Louis and Belleview Mineral Railroad Company was chartered, although nothing was done until March, 1851, when the St. Louis and Iron Mountain Railroad Company was begun.

March 3. The St. Louis Theater Company was incorporated.

April 11. The Bank of the State of Missouri was established.

1838   April. William Carr Lane was elected mayor.

July 3. The St. Louis Evening Gazette began publication. It was the origin of the Post-Dispatch. In 1847 its name was changed to the Evening Mirror.

October 10. The Second Presbyterian Church was organized.

October 15. Kemper College was opened.

1839   A new charter was granted which extended the city limits.

ST. LOUIS

Charles Balmer organized the first orchestra. His father-in-law, Henry Weber, opened the first vocal studio.

St. Francis Xavier's Catholic Church was opened.

September 31. St. Andrew's Society, a benevolent association composed of natives of Scotland, was formed.

1840

March. The First United Presbyterian Church was organized.

April. John F. Darby was delected mayor.

April 20. St. Paul's Church was organized.

November. The Missouri Medical College was opened through the energies of Dr. Joseph N. MacDowell.

1841

The first commercial college was founded.

The first Lutheran parochial school in St. Louis was organized.

The Fireman's Fund Association was organized for the relief of the sick and disabled firemen and families.

February 13. The Catholic orphan Association was organized.

April. John D. Daggett was elected mayor.

November 8. The Friends of Ireland was organized to relieve sufferers in Ireland.

December 28. St. John's Episcopal Church was organized.

1842

The St. Louis Medical College was founded as the medical department of St. Louis University. It was incorporated in 1844. It became the medical faculty of Washington University on April 14, 1891.

The Missouri Baptist was issued as the first Baptist publication. It became extinct in 1844.

William C. Carr donated Carr Square to the City.

The Missouri Free School was established by Dr. William G. Eliot for the instruction of girls.

Mrs. Vital M. Garesche started the first dispensary for free treatment of the poor.

April. George Maguire was elected mayor.

Summer. Charles Dickens visited St. Louis during his visit to the United States.

1843

The German Evangelical St. Mark's Church was organized.

The St. Louis Medical and Surgical Journal was founded by Dr. M. L. Linton.

St. Mary's Girls' Orphan Asylum was founded by the Sisters of Charity.

The Roman Catholic Temperance Society was formed.

Edward Wyman began his English and Classical High School.

The rector and ladies of St. John's Parish organized the oldest Protestant orphanage.

February 8. The state legislature passed an act reducing the law incorporating the city and all amendments to it in one law. The corporate name was changed to The City of St. Louis.

March 28. John J. Audubon arrived in St. Louis to spend four weeks preparatory to his trip up the Missouri River to the Yellowstone to complete illustrations for his Quadrupeds of America.

April. John M. Wimer was elected mayor.

July. The Evangelical St. Peter's Church was organized.

1844

The St. Louis Division No. 1 of the Sons of Temperance was instituted.

The Truth, a Presbyterian journal, was first published as was Der Lutheraner, a bimonthly German Evangelical organ.

Lafayette Park was acquired.

The Fire Wardens association was instituted by an association of gentlemen in the interest of the underwriters to protect goods from injury or loss by fire and water.

February. The Pine Street Presbyterian Church was organized.

February 10. The Mill Boy was published supporting Henry Clay. It ceased publication on January 21, 1845.

April. Bernard Pratte was elected mayor.

April 18. The Fourth Presbyterian or Central Church was organized.

May. Grace Episcopal Church was organized.

June 25. The Convent and Academy of Visitation for Women was established.

July 15. The Deutsche Tribune appeared. It eventually merged with the Democratic Tribune and was suspended in 1852.

1845   The Westminster Church was organized.

St. Vincent's Cemetary was opened.

The Missouri Medical and Surgical Journal, a monthly, was founded. It merged with the St. Louis Medical and Surgical Journal in 1848.

The City Hospital was established.

St. Joseph's German Catholic Church was opened.

March 5. Eden Methodist Church was opened.

March 27. The North Presbyterian Church was established.

Fall. Two theaters were built; one was on Main Street and the other was the National Theater.

October 8. The Polyhymnia Society held its first concert.

CHRONOLOGY

November. The Catholic News-Letter, a weekly, first appeared. It discontinued publication on April 1, 1848.

December. The Mercantile Library was organized. It opened in April, 1846.

1846

The first choral society of men only, the St. Louis Saengerbund, was organized.

A conference met at St. Louis to establish the Lutheran Synod of Missouri, Ohio and Other States.

The Western Watchman, a weekly, began publication.

April. Peter G. Camden was elected mayor.

1847

St. Louis was erected into an archiocese with Bishop Peter Kenrick becoming the first archbishop.

Gas lighting was introduced.

The Chicago, Alton and St. Louis Railroad had its beginnings in the Alton and Sangaman Railroad. The road was finally extended to St. Louis.

The Hannibal and St. Joseph Railroad Company was chartered. It was opened February 15, 1859. It diverted traffic away from St. Louis to Chicago and the East.

The Missouri Bible Society was established.

April. Bryan Mullanphy was elected mayor.

June 21. The Sisters of Loretto established the Loretto Academy for Women.

October 18. The Boatmen's Savings Institution was opened. The name was changed to the Boatmen's Savings Bank in 1857 and the Boatmen's Bank in 1890.

December 22. The telegraph line was opened in St. Louis.

1848

The Hotel for Invalids was established.

The New Era, a newspaper, was first published. It became the Intelligencer in 1849.

The German Emigrant Aid Society was organized.

The Prison Discipline Society was founded to distribute religious literature and do evangelical work among the prisoners in St. Louis County Jail.

Rev. John Higginbotham organized the Roman Catholic Total Abstinence and Benevolent Society.

The Ursuline Convent and the Convent of the Good Shepherd were established.

A steam ferry was established at Carondolet.

January. The Western Journal, a monthly, was published.

April. John M. Krum was elected mayor.

July. The Western Literary Emporium was first issued.

October. The Evangelical St. Paul's Church was founded.

1849   The Merchants' Exchange was founded.

The Lutheran College and Seminary was moved from Perry County to St. Louis.

The Christian Brothers' College, Catholic, was established.

Der Friedensbote first appeard.

St. Louis suffered from a serious cholera epidemic and a bad fire which destroyed much property.

The St. Louis Millers' Exchange was organized.

The City Dispensary was opened.

The following Catholic churches were opened: The Holy Trinity, German and St. Michael's.

April. James G. Barry was elected mayor.

May 31. The Fire Association of all the volunteer fire companies was organized.

October 15. A national convention was called to meet in St. Louis to promote construction of a national Pacific railroad and telegraph line to the Pacific Ocean. It followed the California Gold Rush.

1850

The population of St. Louis was 77,860.

Laws were passed for the issuance of special tax bills to pay for construction of public sewers.

The St. Louis Times appeared.

The Social Saengerchor, a choral society, was organized.

The St. Louis Christian Advocate, a Presbyterian journal, was first published.

The St. Louis Dental Association was organized.

The Deutsche Schule Verein, the German School Association and Free Community of North St. Louis, was founded.

The German Medical Society was formed.

The Carondelet Presbyterian Church was organized.

Eli W. Whelan, a blindman, established the Missouri School for the Blind.

March 5. The Louisville and Nashville Railroad Company was incorporated by the Kentucky Legislature. It secured possession of the St. Louis and Southeastern Railroad in 1880.

April. Luther M. Kennett was elected mayor.

June. Le Courier de Saint Louis, the first French newspaper, was published in St. Louis.

September. The Third Baptist Church was organized.

December. The Fourth Baptist Church was organized.

1851

The Illinois Central Railroad was chartered. St. Louis was connected to it by the Ohio and Mississippi Railroad at Sandoval. In August, 1896, the Illinois Central opened its St. Louis-Chicago Line.

January 9. The Bates Theater was opened.

March 18. Jenny Lind made her first appearance in St. Louis at Wyman's Hall.

June 13. St. Vincent's German Orphan Asylum was founded.

July 4. Actual construction of the Pacific Railroad was begun.

September. The Homeopathic Medical News Letter was started and published for one year.

1852

The Central Christian Advocate, an anti-slavery journal, was begun at Lebanon, Illinois, and moved to St. Louis in 1856.

The St. Louis Herald appeared, the third of that name. It was suppressed by the national government during the Civil War because of its southern tone.

The Lake Erie, Wabash and St. Louis Railroad Company was incorporated.

The Chicago, Burlington and Quincy Railroad (named in 1855) had its beginning in a branch road from Turner Junction, Illinois to Aurora, Illinois. Then the Chicago and Aurora Railroad Company was organized.

The Varieties Theater was opened.

The Botantical Garden was organized.

Lafayette Company No. 1, the only hook and ladder company in the fire department, was formed.

William McKee merged the Argus with the Signal into the Democrat to support Thomas Hart Benton.

Ebenezer McNeil organized the Caledonian Society to keep alive memories of Scotland.

The Western Review was first published.

March 14. The First Congregational church was organized.

CHRONOLOGY

	October. St. Johns Church, Evangelical, was organized.
1853	The Temple of Honor, a temperance society, was formed.
	The Convent Mutual Life Insurance Company was formed.
	The first Young Men's Christian Association in St. Louis was organized. It was disbanded during the war.
	The American Express Company started its business in St. Louis.
	February 3. The Home of the Friendless for aged widows was organized.
	February 22. The Charter for Washington University was granted by the state legislature.
	April. John How was elected mayor.
	April 20. Florence Village was laid out by James S. Watson and Samuel D. Smith. It was later annexed to St. Louis.
	May. The German Savings Institution was opened.
	May 12. St. Ann's Widows' Home, Lying-in Hospital and Foundling Asylum was founded by the Sisters of Charity. It was opened September 8.
	October 4. The Home of the Friendless was organized.
1854	The Shamrock Society, a benevolent society, was formed in St. Louis.
	The city purchased the land for Hyde Park.
	Riots occurred, which the mayor found himself without the authority to suppress. In 1855 the legislature amended the charter to give the city greater authority to suppress riots.
	The Missouri Park was created by city ordinance. The first appropriation was made in 1858.
	The United States Express Company opened its office in St. Louis.

A Bohemian Benevolent Association was organized: the Cesko-Slovansky Podporvjici Spolek.

January 7. The first number of the French journal La Revue de l'Ouest was issued.

February 4. The Girls' Industrial Home for the care and industrial training of destitute children was established.

September. Barnum's Hotel was opened.

1855

The St. Louis Leader was first published.

Missouri Lodge No. 22, first branch of B'nai B'rith, was formed.

The O'Fallon Polytechnic Institute was founded under the auspices of Washington University.

The Sons of Malta, a mystic society, was organized.

The State Savings Institution was established. Its name was changed to the State Savings Association in 1859.

A branch of the Ancient Order of Hibernians was instituted.

January. A run on the banking houses occurred.

February. The Fifth Episcopal Church, the Trinity Church, was organized.

March 10. The St. Louis Leader, a weekly paper, was founded by a Catholic literary society. It became a daily in 1856.

April. Washington King was elected mayor.

November. The first movement was made toward the establishment of the St. Louis Fair.

November 1. A fouteen-car special train left St. Louis to mark the inauguration of service to Jefferson City on the Pacific Railroad.

December 5. The Village of Highland became a part of St. Louis.

CHRONOLOGY

1856   The Bryant and Stratton Commercial College was opened.

The Exchange Bank was opened.

The Industrial School was established by the Sisters of St. Joseph's Convent of Mercy in St. Louis to help small girls.

The Mechanics' Exchange was organized. It was incorporated on September 20, 1875 under the name of the Builders' Exchange of the City of St. Louis.

January 1. The Trinity Methodist Episcopal Church was organized.

March 10. The St. Louis Academy of Science was established.

March 15. The Retail Shoe Merchants' Association was organized.

April. John How was elected mayor.

June 27. The Sisters of the Order of Mercy arrived and began their work of creating St. Joseph's House of Mercy for the Poor.

July 26. The first lodge of the American Protestant Association was founded.

September. The Smith Academy, a high school for boys, was opened.

1857   The St. Louis Bank-Note Reporter, Counterfeit Detector and Wholesale Price Current was first published as a weekly.

The Missouri Railroad Company was organized.

Eberhard Anheuser, principal creditor of the Schneider Brewery whose owners failed in business, took over the business. He eventually took his son-in-law into the firm in 1861. The company was incorporated in 1875 as the Anheuser-Busch Brewing Association. Budweiser Beer was first introduced in 1876.

The German Mutual Life Insurance Company was incorporated, as was the St. Louis Mutual Life Insurance Company.

The Southern Bank of St. Louis was founded. It became the Third National Bank of St. Louis in 1864. The St. Louis Building and Savings Association was also organized. It took the name of the Bank of Commerce in 1869 and later became a national bank. Other banks established under the legislation for a general banking system were: the Merchants' Bank, the Mechanics' Bank, the Exchange Bank, the Union Bank, and the Bank of St. Louis.

1857   April. John M. Wimer was elected mayor.

April 22. Washington University was formally inaugurated.

June. The Pacific Hotel was opened. It was destroyed by fire on February 20, 1858.

August 5. The Westliche Post first appeared. Carl Schurz and Joseph Pulitzer were both associated with the paper for a period of time.

September 14. The fire department began to use steam engines.

November. The Homeopathic Medical College of Missouri was chartered. It closed from 1860 to 1864 because of the war. It then continued until 1869. It was reincorporated in 1880 as the St. Louis College of Homeopathic Physicians and Surgeons.

1858   Dr. William Torrey Harris developed the St. Louis movement of speculative philosophy and art criticism which culminated in the organization of both the St. Louis Art Society and the Kant Club.

The first tribe in Missouri of the Order of Red Men was organized in St. Louis. It was called the Minnehaha Tribe.

Rev. L. E. Nollau founded the German Protestant Orphans' Home.

The House of Refuge was established for indoor relief.

The Sisters of Notre Dame came to St. Louis.

St. Vincent's Institutuion for the insane was established by the Sisters of Charity.

The United States Marine Hospital and the Good Samaritan Hospital were opened.

Eugene L. Massot organized the St. Louis Pharmaceutical Association.

The Evangelical Friedens Church was founded.

St. Malachy Catholic Church was opened.

February 22. The general fire-alarm system was completed.

April. Oliver Dwight Filley was elected mayor.

September 1. The first United States lodge of the Treu Bund, a secret fraternity, was organized in St. Louis.

December 15. The Lutheran Hospital was founded by Dr. Binger.

1859   The Humboldt Institut Oder Deutsche, a German Medical College, was opened by Dr. Adam Hammer. It was suspended during the Civil War, reopened in 1866 and then closed in 1899.

Richard Edwards began publication of Edward's Monthly.

March 19. The Germania Saengerbund, a German singing society, was organized.

April 9. Samuel L. Clemens received Pilot's Certificate No. 596 from the inspectors of the District of St. Louis. He used many of his experiences on the Mississippi River as background and themes for his stories written under the pseudonym of Mark Twain.

May 10. The Missouri Railway Company, a street railway line, was organized. The first car was run on July 4, 1859.

May 11. Mary Institute, a school for girls, was opened.

August 24. The House of the Guardian Angel was founded by the Sisters of Charity of St. Vincent de Paul.

September 5. H.D. Moore organized the Mount Vernon chapter of Temperance and Wisdom in St. Louis.

Fall. The City University was opened.

November 28. The French Mutual Aid Society was organized to aid its members, all of whom spoke French.

1860   The Western Academy of Art was established in St. Louis.

The Tenth Ward Savings Association, later the St. Louis National Bank, was opened.

The Philharmonic Orchestra was organized.

March 3. The St. Louis Provident Association was organized to provide a better system of private charity.

March 19. The St. Louis Law School was organized, but it was not opened until 1867 because of the Civil War.

1861   St. John's Hospital was founded and conducted by the Sisters of Mercy.

The Missouri School for the Blind was opened.

The Ladies' Union Refugee Aid Society was formed to aid refugees from Southwestern Missouri who were dislocated because of the Civil War.

The Myrtle Street Prison was opened.

Mrs. Anne Sneed Cairns founded Kirkwood Seminary which was the beginning of Forest Park University for Women. It moved to St. Louis in 1891.

January. A Committee of Safety was formed to keep Missouri in the Union.

The Union Guards was formed by Union suporters.

March 4. The Convention of the State of Missouri reconvened after a two-day meeting, February 28-29, at Jefferson City, to consider relations between the state and the federal government.

April. Daniel Gilchrist Taylor was elected mayor.

April 14. H.D. Moore organized the Bond of Hope, a temperance society.

CHRONOLOGY

May. The United States Reserve Corps of Missouri was organized.

Summer. The Western Sanitary Commission was organized to develop sanitary conditions for the soldiers.

August 14. Martial law was declared in St. Louis, and Major McKinstry was appointed provost marshal.

August 30. All of Missouri was placed under martial law.

Fall. A system of forts defending St. Louis was completed.

October. The Fremont Relief Society was organized by the ladies of St. Louis to aid sick and wounded soldiers.

1862　　A Franciscan Monastery was established.

The Gravois Street Railway was constructed.

The Soldiers' Orphans' Home was established.

The Union League was formed by staunch Union supporters.

January. The Union Merchants' Exchange was formed by those businessmen supporting the Union who withdrew from the old chamber of commerce, which had some Southern sympathies.

July. John Peckham called a mass meeting in order to express Union sentiment.

1863　　Several charities for the care of Hebrews were established: The Ladies', Widows and Orphans' Society, The Ladies Zion Society, and The Young Ladies' Hospital Aid Society.

The Second National Bank was established.

The German Evangelical Lutheran Orphans' Home was incorporated

The St. Louis ladies founded The Freedmen's Relief Society.

The following German Catholic churches were opened: Holy Cross and St. Anthony.

ST. LOUIS

March 1. Pastor H.C. Cox announced the plan of organization for the Methodist Union Congregational Church.

April. Chauncey Ives Filley was elected mayor.

May 2. The Ladies' National League was formed to aid in suppressing the Southern rebellion.

May 18. The First German Presbyterian Church was organized.

1864

The Bellefontaine Street Railway Company was established.

The Insane Asylum was established.

The following banks were established: the Fourth National Bank; the Union Savings Association, which changed its name in January, 1881, to the American Exchange Bank; and the Provident Savings Institution.

February 1. The Sanitary Fair Association was organized.

February 13. St. Philomena's Industrial School was established.

April. James S. Thomas was elected mayor.

May. The city council passed an ordinance establishing the Board of Water Commissioners. It was organized on March 18, 1865.

June. Rev. James H. Brookes founded the Washington and Compton Avenue Presbyterian Church.

November 3. The St. Louis College of Pharmacy was established.

1865

The Convent Hospital of the Franciscan Sisters was opened.

The Union Street Railway was constructed.

The Walnut Park German Presbyterian Church was organized.

The preliminary organization of the Kant Club, part of the St. Louis movement of philosophy, was begun.

January 6. The Missouri Constitutional Convention met in St. Louis. It passed an ordinance abolishing slavery and required a sweeping test oath of loyalty. It also passed an "ousting" ordinance that removed all county officers and all judges. Governor Fletcher did not remove those officials who were deemed loyal.

February 3. The Missouri General Assembly passed an act establishing the Public School Library Society of St. Louis.

February 16. The Germania Club, a German social club, was chartered.

April 8. The Drake Constitution was ratified by the state convention. Governor Fletcher proclaimed it in effect on July 4, 1865.

July 1. The United States recruiting station in St. Louis was opened.

October 10. Joseph Pulitzer arrived in East St. Louis from Hungary. He became a citizen on March 6, 1867.

November. St. Luke's Hospital was organized. It admitted its first patients in April, 1866.

November 12. The International Bank was organized.

December 5. The Southern Hotel was opened.

POST-CIVIL WAR ST. LOUIS, 1866-1876

1866　　The Missouri Historical Society was organized.

The Western Female Guardian Society was organized to protect women.

A convention was held which organized the Missouri Sunday-School Association.

The Fourth Street and Arsenal Street Railway was constructed.

The United Sons of Erin Benevolent Society was formed by Irish Catholics.

The Atlas Mutual Insurance Company was organized.

The following Catholic churches were erected: the German St. Nicholas and the Holy Angels.

The Laclede Race Track Association was formed. It was disbanded in 1869.

Arian, a singing society, was formed.

March. The Commercial Bank and the Continental National Bank were organized.

June 25. A city ordinance was passed making the old City Cemetery into Benton Park.

June 27. The Missouri Southern Relief Association was formed to aid Southerners who suffered as a result of the Civil War.

July. A fifth <u>Times</u> appeared. It was absorbed by <u>The Republican</u> in 1879.

October 22. The French paper <u>La Tribune Française</u> first appeared.

December 5. The Pilgrim Congregational Church was organized.

1867

The St. Louis Press Club was formed.

J. B. Merwin established <u>The American Journal of Education.</u>

William Bell began publication of <u>The Western Trade Journal</u>. It was discontinued in the late 1880's.

The Orpheus Singing Society was established. It merged with the St. Louis Saengerbund in 1878.

The Grand Lodge of Missouri of the colored Masons was organized.

The Missouri Mutual Insturance Company was established.

The Knights of St. Patrick was founded for Irish members.

The first lodge of the Sons of Harmon, a secret society of Germans, was organized.

The Police Relief Fund was established.

The Mullanphy Emigrant Home was founded to aid needy immigrants coming to St. Louis.

The Board of Trade was established.

St. Francis de Sales, a German Catholic church, was erected.

The Franklin Avenue German Savings Institution was incorporated.

George F. Gouley began publication of The Freemason which was consolidated with The Voice of Masonry in 1874.

May 8. The Women's Suffrage Association of Missouri was established.

October 16. The St. Louis Law School of Washington University was opened.

November 19. The St. Louis Home Journal, a weekly, was first issued. It merged with The Western Commercial Gazette in January, 1872 as The St. Louis Home Journal - Commercial Gazette.

1868 Henry Shaw offered 120 acres of land to the city for Tower Grove Park which was formally opened in the summer of 1870.

The Carondelet Baptist Church was organized.

The Independent Order of Odd Fellows organized a library.

The St. Louis Homeopathic Medical Society was established.

The St. Louis Christian Association established the Women's Christian Home for single women.

The St. Louis Insane Asylum was erected by the county. It was turned over to the city when the latter separated from the county in 1876.

The American Baptist Publication Society established a branch in St. Louis.

March 14. An ordinance was passed approving the construction of the St. Louis Tunnel. It was completed on June 24, 1874.

May. The Young Men's Republican Club was formed.

The Order of the Little Sisters of the Poor was founded.

May 16. St. Paul's Benevolent Society was incorporated.

August. St. Paul's Episcopal Church was formed.

October. The Evangelical Zion's Church was founded.

The St. Louis Bethel Association was organized to aid the work of the Western Seamen's Friend Society in St. Louis.

October 1. The Bremen Savings Bank was opened.

November. The Women's Christian Association was organized for philanthropic work.

December 24. The St. Louis Bank Clearing House was opened.

1869　Professor Louis Bauer organized the College of Physicians and Surgeons.

The Madison County Ferry Company and the Wriggins Ferry Company began to carry cars on track barges across the Mississippi between East St. Louis and St. Louis.

Hiram Leffingwell launched the movement for the purchase of land for Forest Park.

The Little Sisters of the Poor founded the Home for the Aged.

The Missouri Dental Journal first appeared.

Dr. Helmuth opened the St. Louis College of Homeopathic Surgeons. It was closed in 1871.

January 24. The Episcopal Church of the Holy Communion was formed.

March. The United States Congress approved the establishment of Lyon Park if a monument to General Nathaniel Lyon was erected.

March 15. The Mayflower Church was organized.

April. Nathan Cole was elected mayor.

April 12. The Engineers' Club of St. Louis was incorporated.

June 10. Fairmount was added to St. Louis.

July 31. Plymouth Congregational Church was established.

October. The Alexian Brothers' Catholic Monastery and Hospital was founded.

November. The Evangelical Carondelet Church was founded.

Joseph Pulitzer, Republican candidate for the Fifth District in St. Louis to the state legislature, won a surprising victory.

1870   The population of St. Louis was 310,864.

Carondelet was annexed to St. Louis.

Joseph Pulitzer was appointed a member of the Board of Police Commissioners by Governor B. Gratz Brown.

Leonard Steinberger founded the Concordia Club, a social club.

The Free Trade League was formed.

April. Joseph Brown was elected mayor.

May 7. The Order of the Knights of Pythias was formed in St. Louis.

November. A United States weather station was established at St. Louis.

December 12. The Western Rowing Club was organized.

1871   The Beethoven Conservatory of Music was established.

The Sanitary Commission established an ear and eye infirmary which was transferred to St. Luke's Hospital in 1873.

The West St. Louis Liederkranz, a music society, was organized.

The St. Louis and Southeastern Railroad was built.

The St. Louis Society of Pedagogy was established to improve methods of teaching.

The following Catholic churches were opened: the Sacred Heart and the German St. Agatha's.

April 6. The Church of the Holy Innocents was founded.

May. The first number of The St. Louis Ladies Magazine was issued.

The Bank Clerks' Association of Missouri was organized in St. Louis to improve old-age and disabled relief.

October. The United Hebrew Relief Association was established.

1872   St. Mary's Infirmary was established.

The Knights of Father Matthew, a uniformed temperance society, was organized.

The Chess Club of St. Louis was formed.

The following Catholic churches were opened: St. Columbkille's and Our Lady of Mt. Carmel.

The Board of Fire Underwriters, a voluntary organization of fire insurance agents of St. Louis, was founded.

The first Lodge of the Free Sons of Israel was instituted.

The Convent of the Franciscan Sisters was established.

The Laclede Bank was incorporated. It became the Merchants-Laclede National Bank in 1895.

Joseph Pulitzer bought a share of the <u>Westliche Post</u>.

The Woman's Club of St. Louis was formed.

Cook Avenue Methodist Church was organized.

The following singing societies were organized: the Chouteau Valley Mannechor, the Druid Maennerchor, Jaeger Saengerbund, and the Saengerbund of the Sons of Herman.

July 18. The newspaper <u>The Globe</u> was started.

October 1. The Female Hospital was opened as well as the House of Industry for women.

November 3. The German-American Bank was organized and opened.

1873

The following Catholic churches were erected: St. Elizabeth's, Negro, and Our Lady of Perpetual Succor, German.

The American Medical College was organized.

<u>Hlas</u>, a Catholic weekly journal printed in Bohemian, was established.

The Convent, Carmel of St. Joseph, was incorporated.

The Choral Society was organized.

All Saints' Negro Episcopal Church was founded.

March 14. The Lafayette Park Presbyterian Church was organized.

May 15. The Northwestern Bank was opened.

August 26. The Board of the St. Louis Public Schools accepted Miss Susan E. Blow's offer to start a public kindergarten in Des Peres Schools. It was the first in the United States.

October 17. The Cotton Exchange was organized.

December 31. The Westminster Presbyterian Church was established.

1874

Carondelet Park was established.

The Live Stock Exchange was organized.

The Schweizer Mannerchor, a song section of the Swiss Benevolent Society, was incorporated.

Bishop Robertson Hall, a boarding and day school for young ladies, was established by the Protestant Sisters of the Good Shepherd.

The Cass Avenue and Fair Grounds Street Railroad was built.

The Central Law Journal was founded.

March 12. St. Louis Lodge No. 13 of the Knights of Honor, a fraternal benefit order, was established.

March 16. The Bar Association was founded.

May 19. The Underwriters' Salvage Corps of St. Louis was organized.

July 4. The Eads Bridge for trains was opened. It was the first bridge across the river at St. Louis.

1875

O'Fallon Park was created out of Colonel John O'Fallon's estate.

The Grand Chapter of Missouri of the Order of the Eastern Star was organized.

The state constitutional convention produced a new charter for the city.

February. The German Benevolent Society was founded.

February 25. The Marine Engineers' Association was organized as a mutual benefit society.

April. Arthur Buckner Barrett was elected mayor. He died in office and was succeeded by Henry Britton.

May. Special agents of the Treasury Department broke up the Whiskey Ring with headquarters in St. Louis. It was a conspiracy to defraud the government of the distilled spirits tax.

May 12. The first lodge of the Ancient Order of United Workmen was instituted in St. Louis.

May 18. The Globe and the Democrat were merged as the Globe-Democrat.

July. The Soulard Market Mission was opened.

October. The Evangelical St. Matthew's Church was founded.

November. The third and more permanent Young Men's Christian Association was formed.

1876   The St. Louis and San Francisco Railroad took over the Atlantic and Pacific Railroad.

The St. Louis Browns baseball club of the National Association was formed and lasted a few years.

Budweiser Beer was first brewed by Anheuser-Busch.

The St. Louis Railway line was built connecting St. Louis and Carondelet.

The Missouri Ear and Eye Infirmary was established and incorporated.

The Zoological Garden was established in connection with the St. Louis Fair.

The St. Louis, Arkansas and Texas Railway Company was organized.

El Comercio de Valley, a monthly devoted to the development of trade with Spanish-speaking countries, was founded.

The St. Louis Spirit, a weekly, was first published. It was consolidated with The Western Live-Stock Journal in October, 1881. It became a daily in June, 1882.

St. Kevin's and the Holy Name Catholic churches were opened.

The Lafayette Bank was established.

April. Henry Overstolz was elected mayor.

April 22. The first telephone company was opened in St. Louis.

May 3. The first number of The National Tribune was issued. It was a Republican weekly.

June 27. The National Democratic Convention met in the hall of the Merchants' Exchange. Samuel J. Tilden was nominated for president and Thomas A. Hendricks for vice-president.

July 3. The new city charter was adopted providing for a board of health.

October 22. The scheme for the separation of city and county went into operation.

ST. LOUIS -- SEPARATE FROM THE COUNTY, 1877-1914

1877

The St. Louis Amateur Opera was established.

The Obstetrical and Gynecological Society was founded in St. Louis.

The Police Reserves were formed.

The St. Louis Herald, the first society paper, was founded. It continued until 1878.

The first real estate exchange in St. Louis was organized.

The St. Louis Dispensary was established.

The St. Louis Connecting Railway was built to operate in conjunction with the Wriggins Ferry Company on its river business.

February 13. The German General Protestant Orphans' Home was founded.

April 20. The Women's Presbyterian Board of Foreign Missions of the Southwest was organized in St. Louis.

July 22. A mass meeting was held in the Stockyards which led to the outbreak of a strike in St. Louis as a part of the National Railroad Strike. On July 25, the strike stopped all trains on 50,000 of the country's 75,000 miles of track. The strike began to collapse that same day.

December 25. St. Joseph's Night Hospitality was opened as a night refuge.

1878   The St. Louis Meat Shop Association was formed.

The <u>St. Louis Echo</u>, a Greenback paper, was first published, continuing until 1880.

The Coal Exchange was opened.

Delos A. Simpson, a deaf mute, organized a school for deaf mutes in St. Louis.

The School of Design was established.

January. The <u>Evening Post</u> was established. It merged with the <u>Times</u> in December, 1878, which had originally been called the <u>Dispatch</u> and then was called the <u>St. Louis Post and Dispatch</u> and finally the <u>Post-Dispatch</u>.

The Order of the Sisters of St. Francis was chartered to begin Pius Hospital.

February. The Teachers' Mutual Aid Association of St. Louis was incorporated.

March. Dr. Philo G. Valentine established the <u>St. Louis Clinical Review</u> which was combined with <u>The St. Louis Periscope and Medical Review of Homeopathic Medicine and Surgery</u> in March, 1884, under the name of <u>St. Louis Periscope and Medical Review</u>.

April. The Brotherhood of Stationery Engineers was organized.

July 15. The Western Commercial Travelers' Association was incorporated.

September. Kunkels' <u>Musical Review</u> was begun.

September 29. The National American, a Know-Nothing weekly, was first published.

Fall. The first Veiled Prophet Parade was held.

October 13. Bernard Singer donated money to establish the Home for Aged and Infirm Israelites.

November 28. The St. Louis Club was organized by various wealthy people.

December 9. Joseph Pulitzer bought the St. Louis Dispatch. The Post and Dispatch was created by consolidation of the two papers on December 12.

December 10. Joseph Pulitzer bought the Times and combined it with the Evening Post.

December 16. The Order of Mutual Protection, a secret society with life insurance features, was organized.

1879

A revised charter was passed extending the city limits and taking in the town of Carondelet.

The St. Louis Woman's Christian Temperance Union was organized.

The Musical Union Orchestra was established.

The St. Louis College of Physicians and Surgeons was founded.

The first branch of the Catholic Knights of America was organized in St. Louis.

St. Cronan's and the German Holy Ghost Catholic churches were organized.

May 22. The Department of Art was established by Washington University.

August 29. The first number of the Jewish Tribune appeared. The name was changed on January 1, 1885 to The Jewish Voice.

October 26. The Furniture Board of Trade was organized.

November. The St. Louis Children's Hospital was chartered.

1880 The St. Louis Quintette Club was organized to perform chamber music.

The Superintendents' Sunday-School Union was established.

The first electric lights appeared in St. Louis.

The Northern Central Street Railway was built.

The Manual Training School was organized.

The Mississippi and Ohio River Pilot Society was organized.

June 8. The organization meeting of the Memorial Home was held by the Women's Christian Association.

June 14. The Order of the American Legion was introduced into St. Louis.

July 31. The Evening Chronicle was established.

Fall. J. Otten established the St. Louis Choral Society.

September 5. The Spectator began publication.

September 6. The St. Louis Tribune first appeared.

September 11. The Hornet, a cartoon weekly, was first issued. It ended on June 24, 1882.

1881 The Swedish Methodist Church was organized.

The Scientific Association of German Physicians was organized.

The Drummers' Association of St. Louis was organized by businessmen of the city.

The Commercial Club was organized.

The Gentlemen's Driving Club was organized for horse racing.

The Mercantile Club was founded.

The Medical Review moved from Chicago to St. Louis.

The Visitation Catholic Church was opened.

The Order of B'rith Abraham, a Jewish fraternal and benevolent order, was founded.

January 2. The Ladies' Land League was formed to end evictions in Ireland.

March. The Sportsman's Park and Club was organized.

March 5. The first Council of the Order of Chosen Friends was instituted in St. Louis.

April. William L. Ewing was elected mayor.

Spring. The St. Louis Protestant Hospital was organized.

May 28. The Civil Service Reform Association of Missouri was organized.

July. The Compton Hill Congregational Church was organized.

September 10. Havlin's Theater was opened.

December 9. Washington Camp No. 1 of the Patriotic Sons of America was established in St. Louis.

1882   Chris Von der Ahe revived the St. Louis Browns baseball club as a member of the American Association.

The Ex-Confederate Historical and Benevolent Association was organized.

The Missionary Training Home was first started to train foreign missionaries.

The American Law Review, founded in Boston in 1866, moved to St. Louis.

The O'Fallon Dispensary in the St. Louis Medical College was established.

The Henry Shaw Musical Society, a singing society, was organized.

The Baptist Orphans' Home was founded.

June 10. The Round Table, a social club, was formed.

July. The American Nationalist, a temperance monthly, was issued. It became a weekly in 1883 and then ceased publication in 1884.

December 21. The St. Louis Dramatic Critic was first issued. Its name was changed to The St. Louis Critic in 1884, and it became a general local and sporting paper.

1883　　A circle of the Chautauqua Literary and Scientific Association was organized.

The Union Congregational Church was formed.

The St. Louis Exposition and Music Hall Association was established.

February 14. The Wholesale Grocers' Association was formed.

March 8. The American Tribune first appeared.

April 13. The Office Men's Club was organized.

June. The Protestant Hospital Association was founded to provide a non-sectarian free dispensary and hospital.

The Master Plumbers' Association was organized.

July. The Industrial Benefit Association was organized to provide relief for working people and their families.

August. The Butcher was first published. Its name was changed to The Butchers' and Packers' Magazine in August, 1892.

September 7. The Standard Theater was opened.

October. The Grand Avenue United Presbyterian Church was organized.

October 22. The Law and Order League was formed.

December. The St. Louis Training School for Nurses was incorporated.

1884

Dr. Adolf Alt founded the American Journal of Opthamology.

The Friday Thirteen Club, a small musical club, was organized.

April 18. The Martha Parsons' Free Hospital for Children was organized.

May. The Letter Carriers' Mutual Aid Association was formed.

May 9. The Game and Fish Preserve Association was incorporated.

August 14. The Missouri Pacific Railway Hospital was established.

November. The first national convention of the Cattle Raisers of the United States was held in St. Louis.

1885

The St. Louis Polyclinic Dispensary was founded by the Missouri Medical College.

The Dispensary of the Beaumont Medical College was established.

The St. Louis Browns won the American Association pennant.

The St. Louis Butchers' Union was organized.

The Evangelical Salem Church was founded.

The St. Louis Camera Club was organized.

The Academy of Architecture and Building was founded.

April. David R. Francis was elected mayor.

April 5. The St. Louis Fair Association was organized to conduct a series of annual races.

June 25. The First German Congregational Church was formed.

September. The New England Society of St. Louis was organized.

September 14. The new Grand Opera House was opened.

September 15. The Musicians' Mutual Benefit Association was founded.

September 29. The Cote Brilliante Presbyterian Church was organized.

October 26. The Young People's Humane Society was founded.

1886   The St. Louis Browns won the American Association pennant and the World Series.

The Harper Woman's Christian Temperance Union, Negro, was organized.

The Master Plasterers' Association was formed.

The Paint, Oil and Drug Club was established.

The Beaumont Medical College was founded.

March. Strassberger's Conservatory of Music was established.

March 17. The South Side Day Nursery Association was organized.

The Sporting News was first issued.

June 14. Moolah Temple, Ancient Order of Nobles of the Mystic Shrine, was instituted in St. Louis.

August 11. St. Jacob's Evangelical Church was organized.

September. Evangelical Ebenezer Church was founded.

November 9. Mrs. Lucy A. Wiggin opened a free evening school for young girls working in factories.

November 29. The Congregational Club was established.

1887

The St. Louis Browns won the American Association pennant.

The Marquette Club, a social club for Catholics, was founded.

The Knights and Ladies of Industry, a mutual benefit association, was organized.

January 9. The Liberty Non-Sectarian Mission was founded.

January 27. St. Stephen's Memorial Episcopal Church was founded.

January 31. The Farm Implement and Vehicle Association was formed to push social intercourse and communication concerning implements and vehicles.

April. St. Mark's Memorial Episcopal Church was established.

April 24. The first experiments were conducted with electric motor cars in St. Louis.

June. St. Louis Lodge No. 9 of the Benevolent Order of the Elks was founded.

September 27-30. The twenty-first annual encampment of the Grand Army of the Republic was held in St. Louis.

October 2. The Sunday Post-Dispatch was established.

1888

The Knights of Hope, a temperance society, was organized.

The St. Louis Browns won the American Association pennant.

The Water Tower Baptist Church was organized.

The Mining Exchange was established.

February. The White Cross Home for young women was organized.

June 5-7. The Democratic National Convention met at the Exposition Hall. It renominated President Grover Cleveland and nominated Allen G. Thurman for vice-president.

August 8. The United Order of Hope, a fraternal and beneficial order, was established.

November. The People's Presbyterian Church was founded.

November 17. The Veteran Volunteer Fireman's Historical Society was organized in the rooms of the Missouri Historical Society.

1889

The Rachel Obstetrical School was opened. Out of this developed the Women's Medical College.

Immanuel Evangelical Church was organized.

Fountain Park was dedicated by the city.

Arrangements were made for electric lights in the city.

The Salvation Army was introduced into St. Louis.

The Cleveland, Cincinnati, Chicago and St. Louis Railway System was formed.

The Retail Jewelers' Association was organized.

The American Journal of Surgery and Gynecology was founded.

The Spritz Tour Club, a German outing club, was formed.

The Shoe Manufacturers' and Jobbers' Association was organized.

Delos A. Simpson organized the Deaf Mutes' Club, a social organization.

The Evangelical Deaconess Hospital was founded.

February. The Christian Orphans' Home was opened.

April. Edward A. Noonan was elected mayor.

April 23. The Missouri Society of the Sons of the American Revolution was established.

May 20. St. Augustine's Episcopal Church was founded.

June 8. The Bethesda Home for the Aged was opened.

June 15. The Masonic Home of Missouri was opened for aged brethren, and widows and orphans of masons.

October 9. The St. Louis Trust Company was established.

December 5. The Daughters of the Queen of Heaven was organized as a charitable society of Catholic women.

The first electric street railway cars went into operation.

1890 The Query Club was organized for young women to pursue various intellectual interests.

The Aschenbroedel Club for magicians was founded.

March 8. The St. Louis Chapter of the American Institute of Architects was organized.

Spring. The first council of the American Protective Association, a revival of the Know-Nothing movement, was established in the city.

June 16. The Union Trust Company of St. Louis was incorporated.

August 22. The St. Louis Spanish Club was organized to encourage trade between St. Louis and the Latin American states.

October 1. The Grand Avenue Free Dispensary was established in connection with the Marion Sims Medical College.

October 3. The Mississippi Valley Trust Company was organized. It was incorporated October 14.

December 18. The Missouri Baptist Sanitarium was established.

1891 The Norton Express Company was opened in St. Louis.

The following churches were organized: the Carondelet Methodist Church; the Hope and Emmanuel Congregational churches; and the Immanuel, Taylor Avenue, and Tower Grove Baptist churches.

The Working Girls' Home was established to provide a safe and economical home for working girls and women.

Rebekah Hospital was opened.

The Retail Grocers' Association was formed.

The first local branch of the Baptist Young People's Union of America was established.

The South Side Bank was formed.

January 1. The Daughters of the Confederacy was organized with Mrs. M.A.E. McLure as president.

January 15. The St. Louis Southwestern Railway Company, the "Cotton Belt Route," was formed. It received the property of the St. Louis, Arkansas and Texas Railway on June 1.

January 18. The Evangelical Bethlehem Church was organized.

March 1. The Mirror was first published by M.A. Fanning and James M. Calvin.

June 12. The Southern Commercial and Savings Bank was opened.

Fall. The Morning Choral Club was established.

October 1. The Germania Theater was opened.

November. The Children's Home Society of Missouri was organized in St. Louis with Dr. John D. Vincil as president.

The Imperial Theater was opened.

November 27. The Union Club, a social club, was incorporated.

December. The Merchants' Transportation Association was organized.

1892   Wells Fargo and Company Express established its St. Louis office.

The Missouri Dental College was made a department of Washington University.

The Barnes Medical College, founded by Drs. Pinckney French, Charles H. Hughes, and A.N. Carpenter, was incorporated.

The St. Louis Country Club was organized.

January 1. Dr. Bransford Lewis first published the Medical Fortnightly.

January 2. The Young Women's Christian Association was organized.

January 21. The Hephzibah Rescue Home for the aid of fallen women was opened by V.O. Saunders.

April 2. Robert A. Barnes died leaving $1,000,000 for the erection of a hospital.

April 17. The Maple Avenue Methodist Church was organized.

April 23. St. Andrew's Episcopal Church was founded.

April 25. The Riverside Hunting and Fishing Club was established.

August. The Jefferson Bank was opened.

Fall. A Kindergarten Committee was formed which opened the Riverside Kindergarten in 1893.

November 29. The Lee Avenue Presbyterian Church was organized.

December. The St. Louis Branch of the Needle Work Guild of America was organized.

1893

The Women's Medical College and Hospital Association was incorporated.

The St. Louis Yacht Club was organized to promote yachting on the Mississippi River. It was incorporated October 30, 1894.

A Christian Scientist Church was organized by Mrs. Julia Field King.

Mrs. Helen Walraup founded the German Working Ladies' Society.

The Baltimore and Southwestern Railway which extends from Belpre, Ohio to East St. Louis, was organized when the Baltimore and Ohio Railroad system absorbed the Ohio and Mississippi Railroad and its branches.

Frank J. Cabot first published The Women's Farm Journal.

January 1. The Noonday Club was formed for social purposes.

February. Squib, a weekly local paper, was established.

The St. Louis Baptist Hospital was established. It was incorporated May 9, 1893.

February 20. The Evening Dispensary for Women was established.

April. Colonel Edward Butler, a Democrat, was able to help the Republicans win the mayoralty election. Cyrus P. Walbridge was elected.

May 12. The Wagoner Place United Presbyterian Church was organized.

November 28. The Hospital Saturday and Sunday Association was established to bring the hospitals together.

1894

The Central Home of Rest Mission, a cheap lodging for home homeless men, was established.

The Bond and Stock Brokers' Association was organized to regulate the sale of stocks and bonds.

The Funny Fellows, a mystic society, was organized to participate in the autumn festivals.

The Jesus Evangelical Church was organized.

The Missouri State Teachers' Association for Music Teachers was established.

William H. Danforth founded Ralston Purina.

The Coal Dealers' Protective Association was formed.

February 5. The Master Bricklayers' Benevolent and Protective Association was organized.

February 22. The Society of the Sons of the Revolution was established in the city.

February 25. Reber Place Congregational Church was formed.

April 15. The Lincoln Trust Company of St. Louis was founded.

May. St. Anthony's Hospital was opened by the Franciscan Sisters.

The St. Louis Sketch Club was organized.

July 11. The Isabel Crow Kindergarten Association was incorporated.

August 10. The Liberty Athletic Club was organized.

September 12. The Women's Hospital was established.

1895

The Children's Free Hospital Dispensary was established.

The St. Louis Association of Painters and Sculptors was founded.

The Protestant Knights of America was instituted to build an organization of Protestants similar to the Catholic Knights of America.

Dr. C.C. Morris founded The Hospital Bulletin, and Dr. S. C. Martin founded The American Journal of Dermatology.

The St. Louis Music Club was organized.

The Atlas of Dermatology was begun by Dr. A. Ohman-Dumesnil. It was discontinued in 1897.

Dr. W.H. Mayfield first issued Health and Home, a monthly devoted to domestic sanitation and personal health.

The Civic Federation of St. Louis was incorporated to remove or lessen the evils of municipal mismanagement.

The Cross Country Cyclers Club was organized.

The Episcopal Club of St. Louis was founded.

The St. Louis Kennel Club was organized.

January 6. The Mercantile Athletic Club was formed.

January 31. The St. Louis Chapter of the Daughters of the American Revolution was instituted.

February 17. The Progressive Order of the West, a fraternal and benevolent organization, was instituted under Jewish auspices.

February 21. The Gallaudet Union, a charitable, literary and social organization for the advancement of the deaf was founded.

March. The St. Louis Homeopathic Dispensary was established.

The Century Road Club of Missouri was organized to promote the building of good roads in Missouri.

April 9. The Great American Society was chartered.

April 30. The Free Library was opened.

August. The Emergency Home for aged people, infants and children was originated by Mrs. Leta Flint.

August 8. The South Broadway Merchants' Association was organized to improve the business facilities of the merchants of South Broadway.

September 1. The Sarsfield Club, a social organization for young Irish-Americans, was founded.

The Merchants' League Club, a political and social organization, was formed.

Fall. The St. Louis Section of the Council of Jewish Women was established.

October. A second kindergarten was opened at the South Side Nursery.

October 2. The Brick Manufacturers' Association of St. Louis was founded.

October 10. The Missouri Society of the Colonial Dames of America was organized.

November 6. The Academy of Medical and Surgical Sciences was established.

November 22. The American Minute Men, a patriotic beneficiary and military organization was incorporated.

December 7. The Tennessee Society of St. Louis was organized for natives of Tennessee.

1896   A branch of the Patriots of America was established.

The Good Samaritan Homeopathic Dispensary was founded.

The first Lodge of the Knights and Daughters of Dixie was organized in St. Louis.

Kenrick Park was dedicated.

January. The Tuesday Literary Club was formed.

The State Federation of Women's Clubs was organized in a convention held in St. Louis.

January 1. Camp St. Louis No. 731 of the United Confederate Veterans was formed.

January 31. The Master Builders' Association was organized.

February 11. The Wholesale and Retail Feed Dealers' Association was organized.

April 3. The Railway Club was organized.

April 25. The Washington University Alumnae Association was organized by its women graduates.

May 27. A tornado demolished many buildings in the city

June 7. Thomas W. Seymour formed Lodge No. 1 of the Knights and Ladies of Honor in St. Louis. It was a mutual benefit order.

June 16-18. The Republican National Convention was held. William McKinley of Ohio was nominated for president and Garret A. Hobart of New Jersey for vice-president.

July. The Women's Bryan League was formed to assist in the election of William Jennings Bryan for president.

July 23. The People's party assembled in national convention and nominated William Jennings Bryan for president and Thomas Watson for vice-president.

July 23-24. The National Bi-Metallic Party Convention met in St. Louis and nominated William Jennings Bryan for president and Arthur Sewall for vice-president.

September 18. The Century Theater was opened in the new Century Building.

October. The Society of the Children of the American Revolution was developed under the sponsorship of the Daughters of the American Revolution.

October 3. The National Convention of Democratic Clubs was held in the city.

October 14. The St. Louis Society of Accountants was formed.

October 19. Mayor Charles G. Warner, Captain Joseph Boya and others organized the Veterans of the Blue and Gray to bind together those who fought on opposite sides during the Civil War.

November. The Missouri Woman's Press Association was instituted.

November 29. Dr. T.J. Thorpe organized the Thorpe Literary and Scientific Club.

December 2. The Women's Noonday Club was formed as a

club where business and professional women could meet and aid each other.

December 14. The Tyler Place Presbyterian Church was organized.

1897

Governor Lon Stephens appointed Henry Hawes president of the St. Louis Board of Police Commissioners. Hawes then enrolled every policeman in the Jefferson Club as part of a reform movement. He supported the more conservative Rolla Wells for mayor in 1901.

The Salvation Army Rescue Home was opened.

The Interstate Merchants' Association was formed.

Arthur Rozelle formed the Free Employment Department, a special department of the Bureau of Labor Statistics. It was a free exchange of information between employees and employers.

The Daughters of the Republic, St. Louis Chapter, was organized as a political society.

The Missouri Baptist Board of Home and Foreign Missions was organized in St. Louis in 1897.

The state legislature passed an act providing for an elected board of education as part of the work of municipal reform.

The Cooking Teachers' League of St. Louis was organized as a branch of the National Cooking Teachers' League.

The Electric Club was organized as a result of the meeting of a convention of electricians in St. Louis.

January. The Free Dispensary connected with the Baptist Sanitarium was established.

January 7. The Woman's Humane Society was organized for the prevention of cruelty to children or animals.

January 23. The Virginia Society of St. Louis was organized.

January 30. The Ohio Society for natives of Ohio was established.

February 25. The Royal Fraternal Union, a fraternal and benefit order, was founded.

March 8. Wellington Lodge No. 419 of the Sons of St. George, a secret benefit society composed of persons born in England or whose parents or grandparents were English, was instituted.

April. The St. Louis Public Library Magazine first appeared.

Colonel Edward Butler, nominally a Democrat, vigorously supported the Republican candidate, Henry Ziegenhein, for mayor. Ziegenhein defeated Edward Harrison, a Democrat and anti-Butler man.

May 1. The St. Louis Traffic Bureau was organized by the Merchants' Exchange and the Business Men's League for the purpose of aiding the merchants and businessmen in handling traffic questions.

July 14. The Order of Columbia, a beneficiary order, was established.

July 16. The Business Men's League passed a series of resolutions inviting various commercial organizations in the city to establish a Commercial Museum.

October. The Jewish Charities of St. Louis was formed by the consolidation of the United Hebrew Relief, The Ladies Zion Society, The Sisterhood of Personal Society, and the Hebrew Ladies' Sewing Society.

November 1. The North St. Louis News was established by Tobias Mitchell and Daniel C. Donovan. It absorbed The Southside Reporter and The West St. Louis News in September 1898 and became known as The St. Louis News.

November 27. The Teachers' Annuity and Retirement Association of St. Louis was formally organized.

December. The Clean Streets Alliance was formed.

December 18. St. Louis Court No. 4 of the Tribe of Ben-Hur was organized.

1898   The Kenrick Social Club was organized.

The Contemporary Club of St. Louis was organized to bring well-known men and women to the city to deliver talks.

January 11. The Advisory Committee of the Missouri Historical Society appointed a special committee to prepare for the centennial celebration of the Louisiana Purchase with Pierre Chouteau as the chairman.

January 14. The Missouri Naval Reserves was organized under the leadership and command of Lieutenant Felix H. Harnicke because of the imminence of war with Spain.

March. The Dante Club was organized as a continuation of the St. Louis movement to encourage the philosophic study of poetry.

March 26. The Columbia Theater was opened.

August 1. The German-American Mutual Benevolent Association was organized to provide sick and death benefits.

October 18. The Alabama Society was founded by native Alabamians.

November 1. The Franco-American Club was founded.

December. The Jewish Fair was held.

December 11. The Police Veterans' Association was organized.

December 27. The Missouri Commandery of the Order of Foreign Wars was organized with D.M. Frost as president.

1899   John F. Queeny opened the Monsanto Chemical Company. He manufactured saccharin, which was a German monopoly. The firm manufactured other chemicals and survived after the war because the German chemicals were no longer available. After a period of decline because of an excessive inventory, the firm grew in the 1930's and then became international in scope.

The St. Louis Browns, under new owners since 1898, became known as the Cardinals with a change of stockings and uniform trimmings. The team was a member of the

National Association, which had bought the American Association in 1892.

January. The Missouri Rifle Club was organized.

The Walhalla Hunting and Fishing Club was formed.

May. Le Club Française de St. Louis was organized as a social, musical and literary association.

1900   The population of St. Louis was 575,238.

A series of strikes was begun by the new Amalgamated Association of Street Railway Employees.

November. Joel Wingate Folk was elected circuit attorney on the Democratic ticket. When he took office January 2, 1901, he would not accept the assistants picked for him. He also had the grand jury investigate election irregularities, which resulted in the indictment of seventeen Democratic and fifteen Republican election officials for neglect of duty.

1901   April. Rolla Wells was elected mayor.

1902   The new St. Louis Browns was formed as a member of the new American League.

March 14. Joel Folk had city boss Ed Butler arrested on a charge of attempting to bribe two members of the Board of Health to get their votes for the sanitation contract for his firm, the St. Louis Sanitary Company, which had the only plant to reduce garbage by the Mertz process, required by law. Butler was tried in Columbia and found guilty. Folk obtained many other convictions.

October 20. Joel Folk had Ed Butler indicted for bribery in connection with an 1898 street-lighting deal. Yet the Butler-Hawes Democratic candidates for the city offices still won the November elections.

1904   Water clarification began in the city.

April 30. The World's Fair was opened in St. Louis. Every state and territory except one participated. It closed December 1, 1904.

November. Joel Folk was elected governor of Missouri. Every other Democratic candidate was defeated.

1905	April. Mayor Rolla Wells was re-elected.
1909	Glen Curtiss flew the first airplane flight in St. Louis in Forest Park, for which he received a large prize.
	April. Frederick N. Keismann was elected mayor.
1913	April. Henry W. Keel was elected mayor.
1914	The Junior League chapter was formed.
	The Federal League was formed with the St. Louis Federals (called the Sloufeds) as members. Eventually this league merged with the American League.
	February 17. Unemployed men marched on city hall to ask for aid.
	May 28-31. Citizens presented the historic pageant and masque celebrating the one hundred and fiftieth anniversary of the founding of St. Louis in Forest Park.
	June 30. A new city charter was adopted.

ST. LOUIS AND REFORM, 1915-1945

1915	December 7. St. Louis was chosen by the National Democratic Committee for its national convention.
1916	February 29. Negro segregation ordinances were passed by a heavy majority of the electorate.
	March 2. The National Defense Conference of Mayors opened their meeting in St. Louis.
	June 8. St. Louis inaugurated its permanent outdoor theater with a performance of <u>As You Like It</u>.
	June 14. The National Democratic Convention was held in St. Louis. It renominated President Woodrow Wilson and Vice-President Thomas Riley Marshall.
	September 15. Members of the police force were asked to contribute to the Democratic campaign fund.
1917	April 3. Mayor Henry W. Keel was re-elected, along with the entire Republican ticket.

CHRONOLOGY

1918	February 3. Employees of the street car lines went out on strike.
1919	March 9. The St. Louis Retail Liquor Men's Association began attempts to have ratification of Prohibition by the Missouri legislature repudiated by a referendum.
	May 13. The Mechanics-American, St. Louis Union and Third National banks were consolidated as The American's Union Third National Bank.
	September 11. The Missouri Public Service Commission granted a fare increase of eight cents to the street railways of St. Louis for a six-month period.
1921	April 6. Mayor Henry Keel was re-elected.
1922	March 20. W.R. Compton announced opening of the St. Louis Joint Stock Land Bank.
1923	The National Air Race, then known as the Pulitzer Trophy Race, was held at Lambert Field.
	January 25. The school board announced that it might add a pig and a cow to the municipal zoo because many children had not seen either.
	May 8. The St. Louis Federation of Women's Clubs adopted a resolution to cut sugar consumption 50 per cent until prices were reduced
	August 31. Members of the St. Louis Lumber Trade Exchange were assessed fines totaling $96,000 for alleged violations of the Missouri anti-trust laws through open price associations.
	November 19. A monument was dedicated to thirty-two children killed by automobiles during the year.
1924	January 12. Fred Essen, Republican boss, and seventy-three others were indicted for their part in alleged election frauds in the primary of August, 1922, in which Senator Reed won the Democratic nomination.
	February 14. A clean-up campaign against gambling and vice resulted in one thousand arrests.

June 23. The United Street Railways Company bought the St. Louis Motor Bus Company.

1925

January 15. The Federal Farm Loan Board approved the proposed merger of the St. Louis Joint Stock Land Bank and the Southeast Missouri Joint Stock Land Bank of Cape Girardeau.

January 17. A group of New Yorkers bought the St. Louis Coliseum.

April 7. Victor J. Miller was elected mayor.

November 2. A federal grand jury in Indianapolis, Indiana, indicted Arnold J. Hellmich, collector of internal revenue, Missouri State Senator Michael J. Kinney, Democratic City Committeeman Michael J. Whalen, Republican leader Jonas Gehrum and others for conspiracy, in which whiskey was removed from the Jack Daniel Distillery, St. Louis in 1923.

December 23. Gerard Swope gave a $50,000 scholarship fund to the St. Louis high schools.

December 24. A commercial radio station was opened.

1926

January 16. The St. Louis Public Service Company was formed to buy properties of the street railways at a foreclosure sale.

September 24. The Cardinals clinched the National League pennant.

October 10. The Cardinals won the seventh game and the World Series against the New York Yankees.

1927

January 18. St. Louis announced its adoption of Toulouse, France, to preserve its art treasures.

May 27. The city proposed to purchase Charles Lindbergh's plane, the *Spirit* *of* *St.* *Louis*, and to build a monument celebrating his achievement.

September 3. Mayor Miller blocked plans for a municipal airport.

1928

January 21. The new Lindbergh Flying Field, formerly the Lambert-St. Louis Field, was acquired by the city. Installation of lights in honor of Lindbergh was done on February 12.

June 21. A delegation of the St. Louis Chamber of Commerce was sent to France as part of the celebration of the first anniversary of Lindbergh's transatlantic flight.

September 19. The St. Louis Cardinals won the National League pennant. They were defeated in the World Series by the Yankees 4-0.

1929

April 2. Mayor Victor J. Miller was re-elected.

July 1. Plans were announced for a grand opera house as part of the new arena under construction.

August 31. The St. Louis Public Service Company tried out a new system giving a reduced fare to regular riders.

1930

The population of St. Louis was 772,897.

May 14. A seminar of Jews, Roman Catholics, and Protestants met seeking ways to develop tolerance.

September 26. The Cardinals won the National League pennant.

October 8. The Philadelphia Athletics defeated the Cardinals in the World Series, 4-2.

1931

January 7. Mayor Miller ordered construction of the municipal auditorium in order to provide for unemployment relief.

September 16. The St. Louis Cardinals won the National League pennant.

October 10. The Cardinals won the seventh and deciding game of the World Series, defeating the Philadelphia Athletics.

1932

January 25. The Interstate Commerce Commission approved plans of the Southern Pacific Railway Company to get control of the St. Louis Southwestern Railway Company. The merger was completed April 14.

May 5. The St. Louis Post-Dispatch won the University of Missouri Medal of Honor.

May 28. The St. Louis Public Service Company avoided a strike by making a compromise wage agreement with the Street Car Men's Union.

1933 April 4. Bernard F. Dickman was elected the first Democratic mayor in twenty-four years.

December 16. Mayor Dickman announced his support of a $17,750,000 bond issue for public works partly financed by the Public Works Administration.

1934 April 21. The new Municipal Auditorium was dedicated.

April 28. Postmaster General James Farley sealed the cornerstone at the federal building.

September 13. Municipal leaders agreed on a bill for a city income tax.

September 30. The St. Louis Cardinals won the National League Pennant.

October 9. The Cardinals won the World Series, 4-3, defeating the Detroit Tigers.

October 22. The Supreme Court approved the acquisition of the St. Louis Southwestern Railway by the Southern Pacific Railway Company.

1935 September 22. Mayor Dickman gave the golden key of the city to the American Legion National Commander Frank N. Belgrano, Jr., and turned over the city to the Legion during its national convention.

1936 February 28. Nine men were indicted on charges of defrauding the government on bids for the Municipal Auditorium, a PWA project.

1937 February 15. The St. Louis Cardinals and Browns announced they would not play night games in 1937.

May 3. The St. Louis Post-Dispatch won a Pulitzer Medal for public service.

October 20. The movements for lights for night games ended because the St. Louis Browns (American League Club) refused to share the cost with the Cardinals (National League Club).

1938   December 24. Mayor Dickman published a paper on the city's fiscal dilemma and sent it to 180,000 homes.

1939   McDonnell Aircraft Corporation was founded.

September 16. The St. Louis Symphony announced a contest for a new symphonic work by an American composer.

1940   January 31. The St. Louis Browns and Cardinals made arrangements to install lighting facilities for night games.

September 21. Antoni Van der Voort won the American Composer Symphonic Work Award of the St. Louis Symphony.

1941   April 1. Republican William D. Becker was elected mayor.

1942   April 25. St. Louis received the Navy E for oversubscribing its Navy Relief Fund quota.

May 23. The St. Louis Globe-Democrat cut its delivery schedule, and the Post-Dispatch and the Star-Times cut their daily editions as a result of paper shortage due to the war effort.

September 27. The St. Louis Cardinals won the National League pennant.

October 5. The Cardinals won the World Series, defeating the New York Yankees, 4-1.

December 19. The St. Louis Symphony announced plans for free concerts.

1943   April. Aloys P. Kaufmann was elected mayor.

September 18. The Cardinals won the National League pennant.

October 11. The New York Yankees defeated the Cardinals in the World Series, 4-1.

1944   March 27. It was announced that St. Louis University would receive $1,350,000 from the Henry E. Sever estate.

April 5. The Board of Alderman passed a bill permitting blacks to eat in the lunchrooms of the municipal buildings.

June 1. The street car and bus operators struck the St. Louis Public Service Company in an overtime pay dispute halting public service. The workers voted to resume service on June 2.

September 21. The Cardinals clinched the National League pennant.

October 1. The St. Louis Browns won the American League pennant, the first in its history.

October 9. The St. Louis Cardinals defeated the Browns in the World Series, 4-2.

1945

April 4. Mayor Aloys P. Kaufmann was re-elected.

August 16. The St. Louis Paper Carriers Local 450A struck in collective bargaining and union representation issues, halting publication of the Post-Dispatch, the Star-Times and the Globe-Democrat.

September 1. The four striking St. Louis newspaper unions published the St. Louis Daily News. The pressmen picketed in protest.

September 7. The three St. Louis papers resumed publication as the publishers yielded to the printers' wage demands.

POST-WAR ERA AND URBAN RECONSTRUCTION, 1946-1970

1946

May 23. The St. Louis Globe-Democrat announced that it would omit advertising during the railroad strike because of the newsprint shortage.

August 22. Oliver L. Parks gave Parks Air College to St. Louis University. It was known as Parks College of Aeronautical Technology, and Oliver Parks remained dean.

September. The St. Louis Cardinals won the National League pennant.

October 15. The Cardinals won the World Series, defeating the Boston Red Sox, 4-3.

CHRONOLOGY

1947   April 13. The pressmen of the <u>St. Louis Globe-Democrat</u> and <u>Post-Dispatch</u> walked out over their pay raise demands. They defied union president G.L. Berry's order to return. They halted publication again on May 24 and finally accepted the pay raise offer on May 25.

November 25. It was announced that the St. Louis Cardinals and their minor league holdings were sold to a group headed by Postmaster General Robert E. Hannegan.

1948   May 3. The <u>St. Louis Post-Dispatch</u> won the Pulitzer Gold Medal Award.

December 11. St. Louis University formed a Writers' Institute to aid talented students who were unable to finance their education.

1949   January 27. President Robert E. Hannegan sold his controlling interest in the Cardinals to F.M. Saigh, Jr.

April 6. The Democrats won the municipal elections for the first time in eight years. Joseph H. Darst was elected mayor.

April 19. The board of aldermen engaged in a fist fight over the members' seating.

June 22. Mayor Darst appointed a race relations council with Russell L. Dearmont as temporary chariman.

November 19. St. Louis University announced that it would offer work in Arctic biology.

December 6. The St. Louis Cardinals announced plans to construct a stadium seating 52,000. They were having a dispute with the Browns over the use of Sportsmen's Park, owned by the Browns.

1950   The population of St. Louis was 856,796.

May 1. The <u>St. Louis Post-Dispatch</u> received a Pulitzer Prize.

May 28. Mayor Darst commented on the city's financial crisis. Governor Smith was scored for his failure to call a special session of the Missouri legislature in order to have an act passed continuing the city earnings tax.

August 12. Buses and street cars were halted by a wildcat strike of the Motor Coach Employees Union for a seven-cent hourly pay raise awarded by an arbiter. V. Julian was named to operate the state-seized Public Service Company. The strikers returned to work on August 14, after receiving an ultimatum from Governor Smith.

November 25. Plans were outlined for the proposed St. Louis-Kansas City Turnpike.

1951

January 22. As the Teamsters Union and management agreed on an impartial chairman for the wage dispute board, 125 striking bus drivers returned to work.

June 5. The St. Louis Post-Dispatch acquired the Star-Times.

June 21. Bill Veeck got an option to buy the St. Louis Browns (American League Club). It would stay in St. Louis. He assumed control on July 5.

1952

May 5. The St. Louis Post-Dispatch was awarded a Pulitzer Prize.

August 27. The board of aldermen passed a nineteen-month one-half percent tax on corporate profits and earnings of all persons working in the city, including non-residents.

1953

January 28. F.M. Saigh was sentenced on tax evasion. He indicated he would sell the St. Louis Cardinals. Its vice-president, W. Walsingham, was to be acting president.

February 20. August A. Busch, Jr. bought the St. Louis Cardinals for $3.75 million and pledged not to move the franchise.

April 7. Professor Raymond R. Tucker was elected mayor of St. Louis.

April 9. The Cardinals bought Sportsman's Park and renamed it Busch Stadium.

September 29. The American League approved moving the franchise of the St. Louis Browns to Baltimore. A syndicate headed by Clarence W. Miles bought Bill Veeck's interest for $2,475,000. The team was to be called the Orioles.

CHRONOLOGY 63

November 5. Pope John XXIII gave his approval to the plans for the Pius XII Memorial Library at St. Louis University, which was to house microfilms of the Vatican Library manuscripts.

1954

February 23. Senator Edwin C. Johnson introduced a bill, aimed at Cardinals President Busch, to make professional clubs owned by alcoholic beverage manufacturers liable to anti-trust laws, charging that Busch was planning to use the broadcasts of the games to create a beer monopoly. The bill was withdrawn May 26, but Senator Johnson said he would warn all clubs against such a possible monopolistic charge.

March 5. Municipal employees voted to end their strike after Mayor Tucker pledged that a new pay plan would be studied.

October 2. A referendum was passed establishing a standing tax on earnings of individuals and businesses which opened the way for a public improvements program. A $100 million bond issue was planned. The tax was expected to yield $8 million yearly.

1955

March 31. Joseph Pulitzer, editor and publisher died. Joseph Pulitzer, Jr. became editor and publisher of the St. Louis Post-Dispatch.

May 2. Daniel R. Fitzpatrick of the St. Louis Post-Dispatch won a Pulitzer Prize.

August 6. Private interests announced a plan for a $15 million redevelopment project to include apartments, commercial buildings and a park.

December 12. St. Louis University received a $1,087,500 grant from the Ford Foundation, and Washington University received a $2,009,800 Ford grant.

1956

November 24. City efforts to prevent deterioration were discussed. Reforms included a three-way slum clearance, housing and industrial expansion drive.

1957

April 3. Mayor Raymond R. Tucker was re-elected.

July 20. A three thousand acre industrial district was proposed for a city-owned site eight miles north of downtown St. Louis to be financed by the issuance of $25.8 million in bonds by the Illinois-Missouri Bi-State Development Agency.

September 1. Officials and civic leaders opened a drive to form a metropolitan district government.

December 18. Fifty whites refused to attend Central High School after a dispute between white and black girls. Police dispersed the crowd.

1958   June 19. The city received a $38,009,636 federal loan for its urban renewal project.

September 13. The price of the Sunday issue of the *St. Louis Post-Dispatch* rose from fifteen to twenty cents.

1959   February 27. The *St. Louis Post-Dispatch* bought the *Globe-Democrat* building and printing equipment. It announced plans to move in and print both papers although they would remain separate.

April 23. Voters rejected a tax rise proposal. As a result, a $2 million cut in the $35 million budget was forecast.

May 23. Rev. John J. Hicks was elected to the board of education. He was the first black to win a city-wide election.

July 24. A bill was signed doubling the income tax to 1 percent. A $4.5 million revenue rise was expected.

November 3. The St. Louis voters rejected the proposal to set up a metropolitan district with St. Louis County to administer certain services.

1960   The population of St. Louis was 750,026.

March 23. Three hundred city workers struck over pay. The strike ended March 25.

August 28. The board of education acted to reorganize the administration as a result of a grand jury probe that led to indictment of ex-board President McCaffrey and his son. The jury found that some members of the board had improperly used craftsmen hired by the buildings department to do personal work for them.

December 17. The Civic Center Redevelopment Corporation announced plans for a thirty-one block renewal project near the main downtown shopping district, which would include an athletic stadium, a motel, parking facilities, office buildings and commercial facilities.

1961

April 4. Mayor Raymond Tuckman was re-elected to a third term.

April 6. The St. Louis Post-Dispatch announced a price rise from five to seven cents.

October 7. Chester E. Stovall was sworn in as welfare director. He was the first black to hold a top city post.

1962

October 27. The St. Louis Public Service Company agreed to sell its properties to the Missouri-Illinois Bi-State Development Agency for $19,450,000. The Bi-State agency was to purchase fourteen other lines. This was a move toward public ownership of transit lines.

November 6. Voters rejected a merger with St. Louis County.

1963

May 11. A charge was made that St. Louis public school administrators were encouraging a return to segregation by permitting whites to transfer from public schools in their home districts, yet were refusing like privileges to the blacks.

June 18. It was announced that the Louvre would lend the painting Whistler's Mother to the St. Louis Museum for the city's bicentennial the following spring.

July 26. The St. Louis education board adopted a limited open enrollment plan. The black members dissented.

October 9. Rev. John J. Hicks, a black, was elected board of education president.

November 15. Blacks protesting inequality ended their boycott of St. Louis stores.

1964

January 27. CORE asked President Johnson not to take part in the city's two hundredth anniversary celebration because of racial troubles.

February 11. President Johnson signed a bill authorizing production of two hundredth anniversary medals for the city and announced that he would attend the celebration.

February 14. President Johnson attended the two hundredth anniversary celebration of St. Louis. Police arrested eighty-six CORE demonstrators as they began to march toward the president. President Johnson planted a tree to symbolize the city's entry into its third century and visited the Gateway Arch.

June 29. It was announced that the Turner Construction and W.J. Moran companies were to handle the $38 million downtown redevelopment project.

July 6. Five hundred persons, mostly blacks, attacked policemen answering the call of a sick woman in a black neighborhood. Six officers were hurt, and four rioters were held.

October 4. The St. Louis Cardinals won the National League pennant.

October 15. The Cardinals won the seventh and deciding game of the World Series, defeating the New York Yankees.

December 21. Mayor Tucker announced that he would seek an unprecedented fourth term.

1965 March 9. A.J. Cervantes won the Democratic mayoral nomination, upsetting Mayor Tucker's bid for a fourth term.

April 6. A.J. Cervantes was elected mayor.

October 28. The final keystone of the Gateway Arch was inserted.

1966 January 22. The United States Labor Department charged that the AFL-CIO building unions had illegally barred work on the visitors center beneath the Gateway Arch since January 10, when three blacks, members of the Independent Unions Congress, were hired. It asked the Justice Department to act. The AFL-CIO Building and Trades Council denied bias, holding that its members never work on jobs with non-AFL-CIO members.

January 27. Busch Stadium was donated to the Boys Club. The new stadium would be completed in May.

February 3. A federal court heard the National Labor Relations Board petition to enjoin the AFL-CIO Building Trades Council walkout.

February 4. The Justice Deparmtnet filed the first "pattern of practice" suit under the Fair Employment Practices section of the 1964 Civil Rights Act against the AFL-CIO Building Trades Council. On February 7 the federal court issued a temporary injunction barring the council and member locals from trying to stop the contractor from doing business with a company employing blacks.

May 12. The new stadium was opened.

May 21. A $52-million privately financed Mansion House Center apartment-office complex was being built as the first stage in the city's riverfront business district rehabilitation program.

July 9. Civil rights demonstrators announced that they planned to stall cars on the traffic routes to the All-Star Baseball Game in St. Louis.

September 28. Vandals smashed windows in St. Louis after CORE protested the slaying of a black robbery suspect, R. Hayes, by policemen. The coroners called the killing "justifiable." Demonstrations continued in the following days, with CORE demanding an investigation.

October 17. The St. Louis Police Commissioner's Board cleared the detective in the slaying of R. Hayes.

1967   January 25. St. Mary's College, Kansas, moved to St. Louis University and became its divinity school.

February 9. The Gateway Arch won the civil engineering outstanding achievement award from the American Society of Civil Engineers.

May 6. The NLRB ruled illegal the refusal of three AFL-CIO Unions to work with three black plumbers of the independent union on the Gateway Arch.

May 30. The Model Cities Agency received funds to plan a downtown renewal program.

July 24. The Gateway Arch was opened to visitors.

August 26. The Gateway Arch received the American Steel Construction Institute Award.

September 18. The Cardinals won the National League pennant.

October 12. The Cardinals defeated the Boston Red Sox in the World Series, 4-3.

1968   January 24. A black, William Cobbs, received a police award for setting up a loudspeaker which drowned out a speech by Stokely Carmichael in 1967. This had prevented a serious incident from developing out of a volatile situation.

August 17. Adam Clayton Powell, Jr. ended a tour of black areas after members of the Black Liberators appeared armed with rifles. Two members of their group were arrested when they refused to put away their arms.

September 5. Eighteen members of the Black Liberators and Zulu 1200's were arrested on suspicion of arson and firing into police and business buildings after the arrest of Liberator founder Charles Koen, along with four members of his group.

September 15. The Cardinals clinched the National League pennant.

October 10. The Detroit Tigers defeated St. Louis, 4-3, in the World Series.

1969   April 1. Mayor A.J. Cervantes was re-elected.

1970   The population of St. Louis was 622,236.

July 12. Mayor Cervantes issued a ninety-eight page fact book to refute the charges of *Life* magazine on May 24, 1970 that he and others in his administration had business and personal ties with gangsters who were operating in the city. Cervantes had filed a $12 million libel suit against Time, Inc., publisher of *Life*, and D. Walsh, author of the article on May 25.

DOCUMENTS

The documents in this section have been carefully selected to illustrate the social, political, commercial and cultural life of St. Louis, as well as the central position of the city in regard to the trade of the nation, from the early nineteenth century through the 1960's. The most pertinent items from the ordinances, charters and reports of various agencies and departments of the city have been chosen in order to indicate the major changes which have occurred in the governance of St. Louis. Especially important in this area is the pioneering role played by the city in urban planning during the early part of the twentieth century and the manner in which it was followed up during the post-World War II period. Studies of housing, recreational facilities and industrial reconstruction as well as core-city redevelopment are included. Descriptions of the city at important periods of its development are also included. Obviously much more could have been included, but the most important documents were selected due to the limited space.

FIRST CHARTER OF ST. LOUIS, NOVEMBER 9, 1809

The taxable citizens of St. Louis petitioned for incorporation of the town under conditions of the Act of the Louisiana Territory Legislature of June 18, 1808. It was registered by the Court of Common Pleas in Book A, page 334.

(Source: <u>The Ordinances of the City of St. Louis, State of Missouri, Digested and Revised by the City Council of said City, in the Years 1855-6 with the Constitution of the United States and the State of Missouri, and the various Charters of the City of St. Louis.</u> St. Louis, 1856.)

The town of St. Louis was first incorporated on the 9th day of November, 1809, by the Court of Common Pleas for the District of St. Louis, upon the petition of two-thirds of the taxable inhabitants, under authority of an Act of the Legislature of the Territory of Louisiana, passed June 18, 1808, entitled "An Act concerning towns in this Territory." The Judges constituting the Court were SILAS BENT, President and BERNARD PRATTE and LOUIS LABEAUME, Associates. The Charter granted by the Court was the only one under which the town existed until 1822, when it was incorporated as a city. It is to be found in the records of the court, in Book A, page 334, in the following words:

"On petition of sundry inhabitants of the town of St. Louis, praying so much of said town as is included in the following limits to be incorporated, to-wit: Beginning at Antoine Roy's mill, on the bank of the Mississippi, thence running sixty arpens west, thence south on said line of sixty arpens in the rear, until the same comes to the Barriere Denoyer, thence due south until it comes to the Sugar Loaf, thence due east to the Mississippi; from thence, by the Mississippi, to the place first mentioned; the Court having examined the said petition, and finding that the same is signed by two-thirds of the taxable inhabitants residing in said town, order the same to be incorporated, and the metes and bounds to be surveyed and marked, and a plat thereof filed of record in the clerk's office. And David Delaunay and William C. Carr are appointed Commissioners to superintend the first election of five trustees in pursuance of the law."

ST. LOUIS IN 1810

Henry Brackenridge arrived in St. Louis in 1810. He presented a fine description of the city indicating its potential for growth as a result of its ability to make use of the Mississippi, Illinois and Missouri rivers. His description of the suburbs indicates the beauties of the area.

(Source: Walter B. Stevens. St. Louis, The Fourth City, 1794-1911. St. Louis, 1911, vol. I, pp. 86-87.)

Henry M. Brackenridge, a young man from Pittsburg, came to St. Louis in 1810. While trying to choose between journalism and the law he did some writing for publication. His description of St. Louis as he saw it and studied it was graphic. His forcast was the more remarkable because both Ste. Genevieve and St. Charles at that time crowded St. Louis in population, and immigration seemed to be inclined to favor New Madrid. In his "Views of Louisiana" Brackenridge wrote of St. Louis:

"This place occupies one of the best situations on the Mississippi, both as to site and geographical position. In this last respect the confluence of the Ohio and Mississippi has certainly much greater natural advantages, but the ground is subject to inundation, and St. Louis has taken a start which it will most probably retain. It is probably not saying too much that it bids fair to be second to New Orleans in importance on this river.

"St. Louis will probably become one of those great reservoirs of the valley between the Rocky Mountains and the Alleghanies, from whence merchandise will be distributed to an extensive country. It unites the advantages of three noble rivers, Mississippi, Illinois and Missouri. When their banks shall become the residence of millions, when flourishing towns shall arise, can we suppose that every vendor of merchandise will look to New Orleans for a supply or to the Atlantic cities? There must be a place of distribution somewhere between the mouth of the Ohio and Missouri. Besides, a trade to the northern parts of New Spain will be opened, and a direct communication to the East Indies by way of the Missouri may be more than dreamt; in this case St. Louis will become the Memphis of the American Nile."

When Brackenridge made his predictions St. Louis had 1,400 people. This writer said, of the impression he received as he went about St. Louis, first taking the view from the Illinois bank:

"In a disjointed and scattered manner, it extends along the river a mile and a half, and we form the idea of a large and elegant town. Two or three large and costly buildings, though not in the modern taste, contribute in producing this effect. On closer examination the town seems to be composed of an equal proportion of stone walls, houses and fruit trees, but the illusion still continues. In ascending the second bank, which is about forty feet above the level of the plain, we have the town below us, and a view of the Mississippi in each direction, and of the fine country through which it passes. When the curtain of wood which conceals the American bottom shall have been withdrawn, or a vista formed by opening farms to the river, there will be a delightful prospect into that rich and elegant tract. There is a line of works on this second bank, erected for defense against the Indians, consisting of several circular towers, twenty feet in diameter and fifteen feet in height, a small stockaded fort and a stone breastwork. These are at present entirely unoccupied and waste, excepting the fort, in one of the buildings of which the courts are held, while the other is used as a prison. Some distance from the termination of this line, up the river, there are a number of Indian mounds and remains of antiquity, which, while they are ornamental to the town, prove that in former times those places had also been chosen as the site, perhaps, of a populous city.

"St. Louis contains according to the last census one thousand, four hundred inhabitants, one-fifth Americans, and about four hundred people of color. There are a few Indians and metiffs in the capacity of servants or wives to boatmen. This town was at no time so agricultural as the other villages; being a place of some trade, the chief town of the province, and the residence of a number of mechanics. It remained nearly stationary for two or three years after the cession; but is now beginning to take a start, and its reputation is growing abroad. Every house is crowded, rents are high, and it is exceedingly difficult to procure a tenement on any terms. Six or seven houses were built in the course of the last season and probably twice the number will be built the next. There is a printing office and twelve mercantile stores. The value of imports to this place in the course of the year may be estimated at $250,000. The outfits for the different trading establishments on the Mississippi or Missouri are made here. The lead of the Sac mines is brought to this place; the troops at Bellefontaine put $60,000 in circulation annually. The settlers on both sides of the river repair to this place as the best market for their produce, and to supply themselves with such articles as they may need. The manners of the inhabitants are not different from those in other villages; we distinctly see the character of the ancient inhabitants and of the new residents and of a compound of both. St. Louis, however, was always a place of more refinement and fashion; it is the residence of many genteel families, both French and American."

The suburbs of St. Louis at the time of Judge Brackenridge's coming began where Fourth street is today. A favorite walk, which was westward into the country, was described by him. The springs the writer mentioned were not far from where the Wabash railroad now crosses Manchester avenue:

"Looking to the west a most charming country spreads itself before us. It is neither very level nor hilly, but of an agreeable waving surface, and rising for several miles with an ascent almost imperceptible. Except a small belt to the north, there are no trees; the rest is covered with scrubby oak, intermixed with hazels and a few trifling thickets of thorn, crab-apple, or plum-trees. At the first glance we are reminded of the environs of a great city; but there are no country-seats, or even plain farm houses; it is a vast waste, yet by no means a barren soil. Such is the appearance until, turning to the left, the eye again catches the Mississippi. A number of fine springs take their rise here and contribute to the uneven appearance. The greater part drain to the southwest and aid in forming a beautiful rivulet, which, a short distance below the town, gives itself to the river. I have often been delighted, in my solitary walks, to trace the rivulet to its sources. Three miles from town, but within view, among a few tall oaks, it rises in four or five silver fountains, within a short distance of each other, presenting a picture to the fancy of the poet, or the pencil of the painter. I have fancied myself for a moment on classic ground, and beheld the Naiads pouring the stream from their urns. Close to the town there is a fine mill, erected by Mr. Chouteau on this streamlet; the dam forms a beautiful sheet of water, and affords much amusement, in fishing and fowling, to the people of the town. The common field of St. Louis was formerly enclosed on this bank, consisting of several thousand acres; at present there are not more than two thousand under cultivation; the rest of the ground looks like the worn common in the neighborhood of a large town, the grass kept down and short and the loose soil in several places, cut open into gaping ravines."

FIRST CITY CHARTER, DECEMBER 9, 1822

With the growth of the population of St. Louis the people recognized the value of incorporation as a city. The state legislature cooperated in this regard. The city government was created with a mayor and a board of aldermen with the necessary powers. Provisions were made for adoption of the charter by vote of the free white males in March, 1833. Elections for the city officers were to be held within three weeks to two months of adoption of the charter, and all future elections were to take place on the first Monday in April.

(Source: <u>St. Louis, Missouri. Ordinances. The Ordinances of the City of St. Louis, State of Missouri, Digested and Revised by the City Council of said City in the Years 1855-6 with the Constitution of the United States and the State of Missouri, and the Various Charters of the City of St. Louis. St. Louis, 1856.</u>)

AN ACT TO INCORPORATE THE INHABITANTS OF THE TOWN OF ST. LOUIS

<u>Be it enacted by the General Assembly of the State of Missouri, as follows:</u>

1. That all that district of country contained within the following limits, to-wit: beginning at a point in the middle of the main channel of the Mississippi river, due east of the southern end of a bridge across Mill creek, at the lower end of the town of St. Louis, thence due west to a point at which the western line of Seventh street, extended southwardly, will intersect the same; thence northwardly, along the western side of Seventh street, and continuing in that course to a point due west of the northern side of Roy's tower; thence due east to the middle of the main channel of the river Mississippi; thence with the middle of the main channel of the said river to the beginning: shall be, and is hereby erected into a city, by the name of the City of St. Louis; and the inhabitants thereof shall be, and are hereby contituted a body politic and corporate, by the name and style of "The Mayor, Aldermen and citizens of the City of St. Louis," and by that name they and their successors shall be known in law, have perpetual succession, sue and be sued, implead and be impleaded, defend and be defended, in all courts of law and equity, and in all actions and matters whatsoever; may grant, purchase, receive and hold property, real and personal, within the said city, and no other, (burial grounds excepted,) and may lease, sell, and dispose of the same, for the benefit of the city, and may do all other acts as natural persons; may have a common seal, and break and alter the same at pleasure.

2. That the corporate powers and duties of said city shall be vested in a mayor and a board of aldermen, who shall be chosen and appointed as hereinafter directed.

3. That the board of aldermen shall consist of nine members, for the election of whom the city shall be divided into convenient wards, which may be altered from time to time, and new wards established, as the convenience of the inhabitants may require, and the aldermen shall be appointed among the several wards according to the number of qualified electors in each.

4. That the aldermen shall be chosen by the qualified electors for the term of one year, shall be at least twenty-one years of age, and citizens of the United States, and inhabitants of the said city for one year next preceding their election, and shall each possess a freehold estate within the limits of the said city; and whenever there shall be a tie in the election of aldermen, it shall be determined by the judges of the election of the ward in which it shall happen, by lot; and all vacancies shall be filled by election as aforesaid, in such manner as shall be provided by ordinance.

5. That the board of aldermen shall appoint their president and all other officers of the board, shall judge of the qualifications, elections and returns of their own members; a majority shall constitute a quorum to do business, but a smaller number may adjourn from day to day, and may compel the attendance of absent members in such manner and under such penalties as the board may provide; they may determine the rules of proceeding, punish their members for disorderly conduct, and, by the concurrence of two-thirds of the whole number elected, expel a member, but not a second time for the same cause; they shall, at the desire of any member, cause the yeas and nays on any question to be entered on the journals.

6. The stated meetings of the board of aldermen shall be on the first Mondays of March, June, September and December, in every year, but they may be convened at other times, on extraordinary occasions, by the major; Provided, that the mayor and board of aldermen may, by ordinance, alter the times of holding stated meetings.

7. The aldermen shall be ex officio conservators of the peace throughout the city, and shall, within the same, have all the powers and jurisdiction now vested in justices of the peace in matters of a criminal nature, and shall exercise and perform all powers and duties which may be vested in or required of them by ordinance.

8. That the mayor shall be elected by the qualified electors of the city, shall hold his office for the term of one year, and until a successor is duly elected and qualified; when two or more persons shall have an equal number of votes for mayor, or any election for mayor shall be contested, it shall be determined by the board of aldermen.

9. That the mayor shall be at least thirty years of age, a citizen of the United States, shall have resided within the city for at least two years next preceding his election, and be otherwise qualified, as in the case of aldermen; and Provided, that no person shall be eligible to the office of mayor who may, at the time of his election, hold any office of honor, trust or profit, under this State or the United States.

10. That the mayor shall nominate, and, by and with the concurrence of the board of aldermen, appoint all officers within the city which are not ordered by law or ordinance to be otherwise appointed; he shall take care that the laws of the State and the ordinances of the corporation are duly

enforced, respected and observed, within the said city; he shall have power, with the consent of the board of aldermen, to remove from office any persons holding offices created by ordinance; he may remit fines and forfeitures, and grant reprieves and pardons in any case arising under the ordinance of the corporation; he shall be a conservator of the peace within the limits of the city; he shall have power to fill all vacancies which may happen in any office (other than that of aldermen) until the end of the session of the board of aldermen which shall next happen after the vacancy shall occur; he shall, from time to time, give to the board of aldermen information relative to the state of the city, and shall recommend to their consideration such measures as he shall deem expedient; he may, on extraordinary occasions, convene the board of aldermen by proclamation, stating to them, when assembled, the object for which they were convened; he shall receive such compensation for his services as may be provided by ordinance.

11. That when any vacancy shall happen in the office of mayor, by death, resignation, removal or absence from the city, removal from office, refusal to qualify, or otherwise, the president of the board of aldermen, for the time being, shall exercise the office of mayor until such vacancy shall be filled; and during the time he shall so exercise such office shall receive the same compensation as the mayor would have been entitled to; and in case of vacancy, as aforesaid, other than a temporary absence, the person exercising the office of mayor shall cause a new election to be held, giving ten days' notice thereof by proclamation.

12. That the mayor and board of aldermen shall have power, by ordinance, to levy and collect taxes upon real and personal property, within the city, not exceeding one-half of one percentum upon the assessed value thereof, except as hereinafter excepted; to make regulations to prevent the introduction of contagious diseases; to make quarantine laws for that purpose, and enforce the same within ten miles of the city, and within the jurisdiction of the State; to make regulations to secure the general health of the inhabitants; to prevent and remove nuisances; to establish night watches and patrols, erect lamps in the streets and lighting the same; to improve and preserve the navigation of the Mississippi within the city; to erect, repair, and regulate public wharves and docks; to regulate the erecting and the rates of wharfage at private wharves; to regulate the stationing, anchorage and mooring of vessels; to provide for licensing, taxing and regulating auctions, retailers, ordinaries and taverns, billiard tables, hackney carriages, wagons, carts, drays, pawnbrokers, venders of lottery tickets, money-changers, hawkers and peddlers, theatrical and other shows and amusements; to restrain and prohibit tippling houses, gaming, gaming houses, bawdy houses and other disorderly houses; to establish and repair bridges; to establish and regulate markets; to open and keep in repair streets, avenues, lanes, alleys, drains and sewers, and keep the same clean; to provide the city with water; to provide for safe keeping standard weights and measures for the regulation of weights and measures, to be used in said city; to regulate the cleaning of chimneys, and fix the fees therefor; to provide for the prevention and extinguishment of fires; to regulate the size of bricks to be made and used within the city; to provide for the inspection of lumber, and other building materials to be sold or used therein;

to regulate and order partition and parapet walls and partition fences; to regulate the inspection of butter, lard, wood, and the weight and quality of bread, the storage of gunpowder, tar, pitch, rosin, hemp, cotton and other combustible materials; to erect pumps in the streets, for the convenience of the inhabitants; to regulate the police of the city; to regulate the election of city officers and fix their compensation; and from time to time to pass such ordinances to carry into effect the objects of this act, and the powers hereby granted, as the good of the inhabitants may require, and to impose and appropriate fines and forfeitures for the breach of any ordinance, and provide for the collection thereof: <u>Provided</u>, that no tax shall be laid upon the wearing apparel, or necessary tools, or implements of any persons used in carrying on his trade, nor shall the same be subject to distress or sale for tax.

NEW CITY CHARTER, 1843

After the state legislature had amended the city charter several times it was believed necessary that the various changes be incorporated into one act. The selections indicate that the city had grown to include six wards and that the legislative branch had been expanded to consist of a city council of board of aldermen and a board of delegates. The executive branch of the city is also described.

(Source: <u>The Ordinances of the City of St. Louis, State of Missouri, Digested and Revised by the City Council of said City, in the years 1855-6 with the Constitution of the United States and the State of Missouri, and the Various Charters of the City of St. Louis</u>. St. Louis, 1856.)

ARTICLE I.

Of Boundaries, General Powers, and Formation of Wards.

Be it enacted by the General Assembly of the State of Missouri, as follows:

1. All that district of country contained within the following limits, to wit: Beginning at a point in the middle of the main channel of the Mississippi river, due east to the south-east corner of St. George, in St. Louis county; thence, due west, to the west line of second Carondelet Avenue; thence, north, with the said west line of said avenue, to the north line of Chouteau avenue; thence northwardly, in a direct line to the mouth of Stony creek; thence due east to the middle of the main channel of the Mississippi river; thence southwardly, with the middle of the main channel of the Mississippi river, to the place of beginning, is hereby erected into a city, by the name of the city of St. Louis.

2. The inhabitants of the city of St. Louis, as the same extends and is laid out above, be, and they and their successors forever are, hereby constituted a corporation and body politic, in fact and in law, by the name and style of the city of St. Louis, and, by the same name, shall have perpetual succession, shall sue and be sued, implead and be impleaded, defend and be defended, in all courts of law and equity, and in all actions whatsoever; may purchase, receive and hold property, real and personal within said city, and may sell, lease, or dispose of the same for the benefit of the city, and may purchase, receive and hold property, real and personal, beyond the limits of the city, to be used for the burial of the dead of the city, also for the erection of water-works to supply the city with water, and also for the establishment of a hospital for the reception of persons infected with contagious and other diseases, also for a poorhouse, workhouse or house of correction; and may sell, lease, or dispose of such property for the benefit of the city, and may do all other

acts as natural persons; they shall have and use one common seal, and may break, change, alter and make a new seal at pleasure.

3. The city of St. Louis shall be divided into six wards, the boundaries whereof shall be fixed by the city council, and be by the council changed from time to time, as they shall see fit, having regard to the number of free white male inhabitants, so that each ward shall contain, as near as may be, the same number of free white male inhabitants.

ARTICLE II.

Of the City Council.

1. There shall be a city council, to consist of a board of aldermen and a board of delegates.

2. The board of delegates shall be composed of two members for each ward, to be chosen by the qualified voters of the several wards, for one year.

3. The board of aldermen shall consist of two members for each ward, chosen by the qualified voters, for two years.

4. No person shall be an alderman or delegate unless he be a citizen of the State of Missouri, and shall have resided within the city limits one year next preceding his election, and a <u>bona fide</u> resident of the ward for which he is elected.

5. If any alderman or delegate shall, after his election, remove from the ward for which he is chosen, his office shall be thereby vacated.

6. Immediately after the board of aldermen shall be assembled, in consequence of the first election, the aldermen shall be divided into two classes. The seats of those of the first class shall be vacated at the expiration of the first year, and of the second class at the expiration of the second year, so that one-half may be chosen every year.

7. The board of aldermen shall elect one of their number to be president of the board, and the board of delegates shall elect one of their number to be chairman thereof.

8. Each board may appoint their clerks and such other officers, servants and agents, as they shall respectively deem necessary in the transaction of their business.

9. Each board shall be the judge of elections, returns and qualifications of its own members, and shall determine contested elections.

10. The majority of each board shall constitute a quorum to do business, but a smaller number may adjourn from day to day, and may compel the attendance of absent members in such manner and under such penalties as each board may prescribe.

11. Each board may determine the rules of its proceedings, punish its members for disorderly behavior, and, with the concurrence of two-thirds of all the members elected, expel a member, but not a second time for the same offense.

12. Each board shall keep a journal of its proceedings, and, as soon as practicable, publish the same in two newspapers of the city, which papers shall be of different politics, and the yeas and nays of the members on any question shall, at the desire of any two of those present, be entered

on the journal.

13. Neither board, during the session of the city council, shall, without the consent of the other, adjourn for a longer period than two days.

14. No alderman or delegate shall, during the time for which he was elected, be appointed to any office under the city.

15. All vacancies that shall occur, in either board, shall be filled by election, in such manner as shall be provided for by ordinance.

16. Each alderman and delegate shall, before entering upon the duties of his office, take an oath that he will support the constitution of the United States and of this State, and that he will faithfully demean himself in office.

17. Whenever there shall be a tie in the election of aldermen or delegates, the judges of elections shall certify the same to the mayor, who shall immediately thereupon issue his proclamation, stating such facts, and ordering a new election.

18. There shall be two stated sessions of the city council every year, and they shall be held on the second Mondays of May and October, at such places as shall be prescribed by ordinance.

19. Upon the passage of all bills appropriating money, of bills imposing taxes, increasing, lessening, or abolishing licenses, and of bills for borrowing money, the yeas and nays shall be entered on the journals.

20. All bills shall be read in each board on three several days, unless two-thirds of the members, elected of the board, shall dispense therewith.

21. A majority of all the members elected of each board shall be necessary to pass a tax bill, bills appropriating, for any purpose, the sum of five hundred dollars or upwards, and bills in anywise increasing or diminishing the city revenue.

ARTICLE IV.

Executive and Ministerial Officers.

1. The chief executive officer of the city shall be the mayor, who shall be elected by the qualified voters of the city, and who shall hold his office for the term of one year, and until his successor is duly elected and qualified.

2. No person shall be mayor who, at the time of his election, is not possessed of the qualifications required for an alderman or delegate, or who holds any lucrative office under the authority of the United States.

3. When two or more persons shall have an equal number of votes for the office of mayor, the two branches of the city council shall decide the election by joint vote.

4. Whenever an election for mayor shall be contested, the two branches of the city council shall determine the same by joint vote.

5. Whenever any vacancy shall happen in the office of mayor, it shall be filled by election in such manner as shall be provided for by ordinance.

6. The mayor may be removed from office for any misdemeanor, by a majority of two-thirds, on joint vote of both branches of the city council.

7. The mayor shall have power to nominate, and, by and with the consent of the board of aldermen, to appoint, all city officers not ordered by this act to be otherwise appointed; he shall take care that the laws of the State and the ordinances of the city are duly enforced, respected and observed within the city; he may remit fines, forfeitures and penalties, accruing from, or imposed for, the violation of any ordinance of the city; he may fill all vacancies which may occur in any elective office, other than that of alderman or delegate, until the same be filled by election, and in any other office until the end of the session of the board of aldermen which shall next happen after the vacancy shall have occurred; he shall, from time to time, give to the city council information relative to the state of the city, and shall recommend to their consideration such measures as he shall deem expedient for the advantage of the city.

8. The mayor may call special sessions of the city council, or either board thereof, by proclamation.

9. Whenever a special session of the city council, or either board thereof, shall have been called by the mayor, he shall state to them, when, assembled, the cause for which they have been convened.

10. There shall be a city register, city auditor, city treasurer, city marshal, city attorney and city engineer, who, in addition to the duties prescribed by this act, shall perform such other duties as may be prescribed by ordinance; there shall also be such other officers, servants and agents of the corporation, as may be provided by ordinance, to be appointed by the mayor, by and with the advice and consent of the board of aldermen, and to perform such duties as may be prescribed by ordinance.

11. The city register, city auditor, city attorney and city marshal, shall be elected by the qualified voters for the office of mayor, aldermen and delegates; and the city engineer and city treasurer shall be appointed by the mayor, by and with the advice and consent of the board of aldermen; they shall hold their offices for one year, and until their successors are duly qualified. . . .

13. It shall be the duty of the city auditor to prescribe the mode of keeping stating and rendering all accounts, unless otherwise provided by ordinance, between the city and any person or body corporate.

14. It shall be the duty of the city treasurer to receive and keep the money of the city, and to pay out the same on warrants drawn by the auditor.

15. The city marshal shall, within the city, in matters of a criminal nature, arising under any law of the State, possess the same powers, perform the same duties, and receive the same compensation as either constable of St. Louis township; he shall execute and return all process issued by the mayor, recorder, any alderman or justice of the peace, under this act, or any ordinance of the city.

16. It shall be the duty of the city engineer to superintend the construction of all public works ordered by the city; to make out plans and estimates thereof, and to contract for the execution of the same; and to perform all surveying and engineering ordered by the city; <u>Provided, however</u>, such plans and contracts shall be first approved by the two boards of the council, or they shall not be valid.

CREATION OF A SEWAGE SYSTEM, MARCH 12, 1849

As the city grew it was found necessary to begin construction of a sewage system. The city government was given the right to create such a system by an act of the state legislature when a majority of the people residing in a section petitioned for it. Provisions were made to permit the municipality to borrow the sums of money needed.

(Source: <u>The Ordinances of the City of St. Louis, State of Missouri, Digested and Revised by the City Council of said City, in the years 1855-6 with the Constitution of the United States and the State of Missouri, and the various Charters of the City of St. Louis</u>. St. Louis, 1856.)

AN ACT TO PROVIDE A GENERAL SYSTEM OF SEWERAGE IN THE CITY OF ST. LOUIS

Be it enacted by the General Assembly of the State of Missouri, as follows:

1. The mayor and city council of St. Louis shall cause, by ordinance, the city to be laid off into district to be drained by principal and lateral or tributary sewers, having reference to a general plan of drainage by sewers for the whole city, and number and record the same.

2. Whenever a majority of the owners of real estate within any district, the city council shall have power by ordinance to levy and collect a special tax on the real estate within said district so drained, not to exceed one-half of one per centum per annum on the assessed value of said real estate, for the purpose of constructing said sewers, which tax shall be annually levied and collected as other city taxes, and shall constitute a lien on the real estate on which it is assessed; and shall not be repealed or altered until the debt created thereby shall have been fully paid.

3. Whenever a petition signed as aforesaid is presented to the city council, they shall provide by ordinance for the letting and construction of the sewers, or such parts thereof as shall be necessary, and may, from time to time, extend, enlarge or alter the same under such terms, and on such conditions as they may deem necessary.

4. The mayor and city council, upon the presentation of a petition as aforesaid, may borrow any sum of money necessary for the construction of the sewers in any district, and issue the bonds of the city for the same, payable and predicated, in interest and principal, upon the tax in the second section of this act mentioned.

5. All moneys, collected under and by virtue of this act, shall be applied to the district from which it is so collected, and to no other purpose or use.

This act to take effect from its passage.
Approved, March 12, 1849.

EXTENSION OF CITY LIMITS -- CHARTER OF 1870

In 1870 the city of St. Louis had grown appreciably in size as well as in facilities. Consequently the state legislature passed an act revising the city charter and extending its limits in order to provide for greater efficiency in government and provision for the needs of its citizens. The selection printed below indicates the new city boundaries and the twelve wards as well as indicating the services which were to be provided.

(Source: <u>An Act of Missouri to Revise the Charter of the City of St. Louis, and to Extend the Limits Thereof</u>. Approved March 4, 1870. St. Louis, 1870.)

<u>Be it enacted by the General Assembly of the State of Missouri, as follows:</u>

ARTICLE I.

CORPORATE POWERS, BOUNDARIES AND WARDS.

Section 1. The inhabitants of all that district of country situated in the county of St. Louis, embraced within the limits prescribed in the next succeeding section, shall be and continue a body corporate by the name and style of "The City of St. Louis," and by that name shall have perpetual succession, shall sue and be sued, implead and be impleaded, defend and be defended in all courts of law and equity, and in all actions whatsoever; may purchase, receive and hold property, real and personal, within said city and also hold the like beyond the limits of the city, to be used for the burial of the dead of the city; also for the erection of water-works to supply the city with water, and also for the establishment of a hospital or hospitals for the reception of persons infected with contagious and other diseases; also for a poorhouse or poorhouses, workhouse, houses of correction, or for any other purposes, and may sell, lease or dispose of any property for the benefit of the city; and may receive bequests, gifts and donations of all kinds of property, within or without the city, in fee simple or in trust, for charitable or other purposes, and may do all acts necessary to carry out the purposes of such bequests, gifts and donations, with power to manage, sell, lease, or otherwise dispose of the same: They may have and use one common seal, and may break, change or alter the same at pleasure.

Sec. 2. The corporate limits of said city shall comprise all that district of country situated in the county of St. Louis, to-wit: Beginning at a point in the middle of the main channel of the Mississippi river, where the continuation of Keokuk street would intersect said main channel; thence westwardly by the said line of the south side of Keokuk street to a point six hundred and sixty feet west of Grand avenue; thence northwardly on a line parallel with Grand avenue, at a distance of six hundred and sixty feet therefrom, until it intersects the Bellefontaine road; thence northeast to the line dividing townships forty-five and forty-six north, range seven, east; thence eastwardly with said line and in the same direction to the middle of the main channel of the Mississippi river; thence southwardly, and with the meanderings of the main channel of said river to the place of beginning; and also the following district of country situated in St. Louis county, towit: Beginning at a point in the middle of the main channel of the Mississippi river, where the continuation of Keokuk street eastwardly would intersect the said main channel (being the same point of beginning as hereinbefore set forth); thence westwardly by the said line of the south side of Keokuk street to a point six hundred and sixty feet west of Grand avenue; thence southwardly in a straight line until said line intersects the northwestern corner of the boundary line of the City of Carondelet; thence southwardly along the western boundary line of the City of Carondelet to the southwestern corner of the said City of Carondelet; thence eastwardly along the southern boundary line of the City of Carondelet to the middle of the main channel of the Mississippi river; thence northwardly with the meanderings of said main channel to the place of beginning. The district of country first above described shall be known as the "old limits," and that last above described shall be known as the "new limits," and they shall be subject to all the provisions hereinafter provided for the government of and improvement in the said "old" and "new" limits, respectively. That part of the city defined and designated by an act entitled "An act to revise the city charter of the City of St. Louis, approved March 13th, 1867," as the old limits shall hereafter be known as the first district; that part of the city therein defined as the new limits shall be known as the second district, and that part which is added to the city by this act shall be known and designated as the third district.

Sec. 3. The said city shall be divided into not less than twelve wards, the boundaries of which shall be fixed by city ordinance, and shall be so established that the population of the several wards shall, as near as practicable, be equal; <u>provided</u>, that until the re-establishment of the boundaries of the wards, as heretofore required, the "new limits" shall belong to and form part of the first ward. . . .

THE FUTURE GREAT CITY OF THE WORLD, 1875

St. Louis has always found itself in competition with Chicago. This urban rivalry was typical of the nineteenth century urban scene in the United States. The following selection discusses some aspects of this rivalry.

(Source: L.U. Reavis, <u>Saint Louis: The Future Great City of the World</u>, St. Louis, 1875).

The great cities of the world were not built in a day. The populous cities of the ancient world were, indeed, situated in the fertile valleys of great rivers, and far from the sea -- as Thebes and Memphis on the Nile, Ayodha on the Ganges, and Babylon and Nineveh on the plains of Mesopotamia; and some others again, like the primeval Sogd and Balkj, upon elevated interior plateaus. They were the work of centuries, and some of them survived the vicissitudes of several thousand years. The strides of the central marts of European commerce from Alexandria to Venice, to Lisbon, to Amsterdam, to London, are measured by periods of centuries. Population and trade move at more rapid rates in our time. Imagination easily leaps over a thousand years. It is not impossible that our City of St. Louis may be "the future great city of the world," but if we are to come to practical facts for our day and generation, and take the safe and sure way, I think we may be content to set it down as both the present and future great city of the Mississippi Valley.

The first leading feature that impresses me is this: that St. Louis is a central mart, seated on the great southern water line of transport and traffic, by the river, the gulf, and the ocean; and that Chicago is another, less central or quite eccentric, situated at the end of the great northern line line of traffic and travel, by the lakes, canals and rivers to the sea. Both are, and will be, great centers for internal distribution; but St. Louis is, or will be, in all the future, in this, the more central and important of the two. For exportation of products, Chicago has been, of recent years, the greater in quantity and value; but St. Louis, in this, has of late rapidly approached her, and in the near future may be expected even to surpass the City of the Lakes. Both reach out over the vast, fertile areas extending from the Alleghanies to the Rocky Mountains and beyond, and from the northern boundary to the Gulf of Mexico, to grasp in the growing trade of the Valley, both of import and export. Chicago reaches out by railroads; St. Louis by both railroads and rivers. And here it may be well to mark the changes that have taken place in the last thirty-five years or so. . . .

In the meantime, while the incubus of war is scarcely yet lifted, and many people are but half awake to the coming future, still dozing in the penumbra of the depression period (as if it were to last forever), St. Louis, I observe, has run out several important spokes of the great railroad wheel whereof she is the hub, or they have been run into St. Louis, stretching southeast, southwest, northwest, northeast, and north -- to nearly all points of the compass -- and when all are completed that are now in progress, or in prospect at no very distant day, they will present the wondrous spectacle of long lines of railroad radiating from the centre to the circumference, not merely of this valley but of the whole United States. It is even now made apparent to any one, by a glance at your map, showing the direction of the more prominent lines of railroad, that such another railroad centre as St. Louis is now, or is fast becoming, is not possible on the map of the United States.

So extensive a system of railroads cannot be completed in a day. The wonder is, that so much has been done in the short period since the war. It matters little whether it be the work of St. Louis capital or of foreign capital. Commercially, St. Louis is scarcely one generation old. In the Eastern cities are the accumulations of one or two centuries. . . .

Consider, now, what is to be the state of things, particularly with reference to the States lying northwest of the Mississippi River (for in other directions the matter is to need special comment), when the system of railroads is completed. The distances by railroad will be, in general, shorter to St. Louis than to Chicago. The radiation of railroads will be somewhat analogous to the radiation of rivers, and St. Louis will have both systems in conjunction; for the longer railroads, as naturally as the rivers, and by the same exigencies of trade and commerce, tend to concentration into one common centre at the great metropolitan city of the West. Here we come upon matters that lie peculiarly within the knowledge and experience of mercantile men. If I may hazard an opinion, I should say that there will be in this quarter a divided empire, with field enough for both competitors, and that the division will be much according to kind of merchandise and the sources whence it comes. Many kinds may reach that region more readily by the great Northern water route and the railroads from Chicago, while many other kinds will be obtained to greater advantage from the St. Louis market -- as, for instance, our own manufactures, and many importations of European manufactures and products, the heavy groceries from the West Indies and Brazil, and teas and silks from China and Japan. Various articles that are brought from distant parts of the globe in sailing vessels will continue to be imported almost exclusively into the Atlantic cities, where the necessary capital is, and where these vessels are built and owned, and these articles will reach the interior of the Northwest more easily by the northern water route than by railroads across the Alleghanies; they cannot be imported from Europe, I presume, because they cannot pay one duty going into Europe, and another duty coming into America from Europe. But manufactures and products of the States of Europe can be imported directly into St. Louis as well as into the Atlantic cities, when regular lines of steamships are established between European ports and New Orleans.

The data furnished by experienced men demonstrate that the bulky produce of the country tributary to St. Louis can go from here to Liverpool by the great Southern water route in bulk, cheaper than it can possibly be carried across the country by railroad to be employed in the immediate business of the city. . . .

REVISED CITY CHARTER, JULY 3, 1876

As the city prepared for the separation of the city and county government, the charter was revised to provide for a more efficient and effective government. The health department was created at this time. Its duties included elimination of unsanitary conditions, registration of births, marriages and deaths, supervision of hospitals, removal of all health nuisances, establishment of regulations to prevent the spread of epidemics, and supervision over deaths and burials.

(Source: The Revised Ordinance, City of St. Louis, No. 17188 . . . In Connection with which are Published . . . the Charter of the City . . . St. Louis, 1895.)

ARTICLE XII.

HEALTH DEPARTMENT.

SECTION 1. There is hereby created a Health Department of the City of St. Louis, which shall be managed, directed and controlled as provided by this Charter and by ordinances of the City of St. Louis, by a Board of Health as hereinafter provided, and by an officer who shall be denominated the Health Commissioner. He shall be appointed by the Mayor, by and with the approval of the Council, and shall perform such duties as may be provided by this Charter and by ordinance. He shall hold his office for the term of four years, and until his successor is duly qualified, be subject to removal by the Mayor as other officers, and shall possess the same qualifications as the Mayor, and shall give bond in such sum as shall be ordained by the Assembly, with at least two sufficient sureties for the faithful performance of his duties.

SEC. 2. There is also hereby created a Board of Health, which shall consist of the Mayor (who shall be its presiding officer), the presiding officer of the Council, a Commissioner of Police, to be designated by the Mayor, and two regular practicing physicians, who shall possess the same qualifications as the Mayor. The Health Commissioner shall be a member of said Board, and, in the absence of the Mayor, the presiding officer. The Board shall meet twice in each week during the year. They may be convened in special session at any time by the Mayor, Health Commissioner, or by any two members of the Board upon written notification served twelve hours before the date of said meeting. Three members of the Board shall constitute a quorum for the transaction of business, and it shall have power to adopt rules and regulations for its government.

SEC. 3. The Health Commissioner shall have general supervision over the public health of said city, and see that its regulations, and the laws and ordinances of said city in relation thereto, are enforced and observed, and for that purpose he is authorized and empowered to make such rules and regulations, with the approval of the Board, not inconsistent with this Charter or any city ordinance or law of this State, as will tend to preserve and promote the health of said city; to appoint such employes, with the approval of the Board of Health, as may be necessary for the execution of his orders; to enter into or authorize and require any employe or police officer to enter into and examine in the daytime, all buildings, lots and places of every description within the city, and to ascertain and report to him the condition thereof, so far as the public health may be affected by it; to declare and abate nuisances in such manner as may be provided herein, or by ordinance; but all condemnations must first be approved by the Board of Health, whose action thereon shall be final. He shall obey all orders not inconsistent with this Charter and city ordinances, emanating from the Board of Health, and shall annually report to the Mayor the general operations of his department during the year then ended, with such suggestions for the improvement of the same as he shall consider expedient.

SEC. 4. It is made the duty of all police officers to observe the sanitary condition of their districts, and through the Chief of Police to report to the Health Commissioner promptly any nuisance or accumulate filth fo found to exist in any portion of the city. The Health Commissioner shall provide for the registration of all births, deaths and marriages occurring within the city; shall have charge of all city hospitals, quarantine, insane asylums, morgue and city dispensary, and with the advice and counsel of said Board of Health make all necessary rules for the government thereof.

SEC. 5. There shall be a Superintendent of the City Hospital, a Superintendent of the Female Hospital, a Superintendent of the Insane Asylum, and a Superintendent of Quarantine when necessary, who shall perform their duties under the general supervision of the Health Commissioner, and shall be appointed by the Mayor, with the approval of the Board of Health; but all other employes shall be appointed by the Health Commissioner, and approved by the Board of Health, except such as may be temporarily in the employ of the Health Commissioner. . . .

SEC. 7. All contracts for work contemplated by this section on which special tax-bills are to be issued, shall be entered into by the President of the Board of Public Improvements, in the name of the city, based on the estimates of the cost by the President of the Board of Public Improvements, accompanied by reports of surveys and profiles, in cases requiring the same in the judgment of such President, and shall be approved by the Mayor and registered in the office of the Comptroller.

SEC. 8. Whenever it shall come to the knowledge of the Mayor that any malignant, infectious or contagious disease or epidemic is prevalent in the city, or will probably become so, he may make proclamation of such fact to the inhabitants; and after such proclamation the Health Commissioner, with the approval of the Board of Health, may have power, by order, to take all steps and use all measures necessary to avoid, suppress, or mitigate such disease, without the intervention of the Assembly, in the same manner and as effectually as the Assembly could itself do by ordinance; and may employ such officers, agents, servants and assistants, establish temporary hospitals, provide necessary furniture, medical attendance and nurses, as in the opinion of the said Commissioner, with the advice and counsel of said Board of Health, may be necessary and advisable: <u>Provided</u>, That the amount expended shall not exceed the appropriation for Health Department. The Health Commissioner shall have and exercise such power until he shall declare, or until the Mayor shall proclaim, that the epidemic or disease, in view of which the proclamation was made, is no longer imminent or prevalent, whereupon the said power shall cease.

SEC. 9. Said Health Commissioner shall keep a record of his acts and orders; shall file all petitions, documents and papers belonging to the office, and shall keep a correct account in full of all receipts and expenditures, and shall make rules and regulations for the government of his subordinates. Copies of such records, documents, rules and regulations, when authenticated by his clerk, shall be presumptive evidence in any court of justice of the facts therein contained: <u>Provided</u>, such rules and regulations are not inconsistent with this Charter or ordinances. . . .

SEC. 10. For the purpose of carrying the provisions of this article into effect, every physician who may practice medicine in the City of St. Louis Louis shall, when a patient dies under his care, make out two certificates, stating the name, age, sex, color and place of birth, and place and date of death, together with the name of the disease of which said person died, one of which he shall, without delay, deposit in the office of said Health Commissioner, and the other he shall give to the undertaker of the funeral, to be delivered by him to the person who has control of the graveyard in which the body is buried. And if any physician or undertaker refuse or omit to do as aforesaid, he shall forfeit and pay five dollars to the use of the City of St. Louis, to be recovered as provided for in section twelve of this article.

SEC. 11. All overseers, sextons, or other persons who may have control over public graveyards in the City of St. Louis, shall make a weekly report to the Health Commissioner of all interments during the week in the graveyard whereof they are such overseer or sexton respectively. Said report shall specify the names and ages of the persons interred, sex, color and place of birth, and place and date of death, and also the diseases of which said persons died.

SEC. 12. If any overseer, sexton, or other person having control of a graveyard, shall permit any person to be interred in said graveyard without a certificate stating the name, age, sex, color, place of birth, place and date of death, together with the disease of which said person died, signed by the physician who attended said person, he shall forfeit and pay a sum not less than five nor more than twenty dollars, to be recovered as in other cases of misdemeanor, before any court or officer having competent jurisdiction.

SCHEME FOR SEPARATION OF THE GOVERNMENTS OF THE CITY AND COUNTY OF ST. LOUIS, OCTOBER 22, 1876

As the city and county grew in population, the residents of both areas indicated a desire to separate their respective governments in order to more efficiently administer the units. The following selection illustrates the methods by which the city and county effected their separation.

(Source: The Revised Ordinance, City of St. Louis. No. 17188 . . . In Connection with which are Published. . . the Scheme of Separation of the County and City of St. Louis. . . St. Louis, 1895.)

Scheme
For the Separation and Reorganization of the Governments of the
City and County of St. Louis, and the Adjustment of Their Relations

The following Scheme for the separation of the governments of St. Louis city and county, the definition of the boundaries of said city as enlarged, the reorganization of the government of said county, and the adjustment of the relations between said city and county so that they shall hereafter be independent of each other, is hereby adopted as organic law thereof:

Section 1. Boundaries of the city of St. Louis. -- The boundaries of the city of St. Louis are hereby enlarged, settled and established as follows: The corporate limits of the city of St. Louis shall comprise all that district of country situated in the county of St. Louis and state of Missouri, to wit: Beginning at a point in the middle of the main channel of the Mississippi river, and running thence westwardly at right angles to said channel, to a point on the west bank of said river 200 feet south of the center of the mouth of the River des Peres; thence westwardly and parallel to the center of the River des Peres, and 200 feet south thereof, to the eastern line of the Lemay ferry road; thence westwardly to a point in the west line of said Lemay ferry road at its intersection with the center of the Weber road; thence westwardly along the center of the Weber road to its intersection of the east line of lot one of the Carondelet commons, south of the River des Peres; thence westwardly to the southeast corner of Rudolph Overman's or northeast corner of B. H. Haar's land; thence westwardly to said Haar's northwest corner; thence northwestwardly to a point in the center of the Gravois road six hundred feet wouthwardly from the center of the bridge across the River des Peres; thence northwestwardly to the southeast corner of lot thirty-one of the subdivision in the McKenzie tract, in United States survey one thousand nine hundred and fifty-three; thence northwestwardly in continuance of said last-mentioned line to the southern line of lot twenty-one of the subdivision of the said McKenzie tract; thence northwestwardly to to a point in the southern line of United States survey 2035, twenty-six chains eastward from the southwest corner of said survey; thence northwardly to a point in the north line of the subdivision of East Laclede, six hundred feet west of the McCausland road; thence northwardly and parallel with the center of the McCausland road, to a point on the Clayton road six hundred feet west of its intersection with the McCausland road; thence northwardly and parallel with the Skinker road, and six hundred feet west thereof, to its intersection with the old Bonhomme road;;thence northeastwardly to the intersection of the center lines of McLaren avenue and Mead street; thence in a northeastwardly direction to a point in the Bellefontaine road six hundred feet north of its intersection with the Columbia bottom road; thence northwardly and parallel with center line of the Columbia bottom road to the northern boundary line of the United States survey number on hundred and fourteen; thence eastwardly along said line to the center of the main channel of the Mississippi river; thence with the meanderings of said channel southwardly to the point of beginning; and the residue of what now constitutes the county of St. Louis shall hereafter be called St. Louis county.

Sec. 2. City and county declared separated; authority of county court annulled. -- The city of St. Louis, as described in the preceding section, and the residue of St. Louis county, as said county is now constituted by law, are hereby declared to be distinct and separate municipalities, and all authority heretofore exercised by the county court of St. Louis county, or any officer of said county, is hereby forever abrogated and annulled, except for the purposes and in the cases as hereinafter provided.

Sec. 3. Election of officers for St. Louis county -- judicial and representative districts established -- county seat. -- At the general election for state and other officers, on the Tuesday next following the first Monday in November, 1876, and every two years thereafter, there shall be elected officers for St. Louis county, as follows: A sheriff, who shall be <u>ex officio</u> collector, coroner, assessor, treasurer; a clerk of the county court, who shall be <u>ex officio</u> recorder of deeds; they shall hold their offices for the term of two years, and shall perform such duties as are now provided by law for such officers, until their successors are duly elected and qualified; also a public administrator, who shall be elected at said election, and every four years thereafter, and shall hold his office for four years, and perform the duties now prescribed by law. There shall also be elected at said election three justices of the county court, who shall constitute the county court of said county, and their powers, duties and terms of office shall be as defined and governed by the general law at present applying to other counties in this state. And for that purpose the county of St. Louis, as established by this Scheme, shall be divided into two districts by a line commencing at a point where the Clayton road intersects the boundary between the city and county of St. Louis as established by this Scheme and Charter, and running thence westwardly with the Clayton road to the eastern boundary of Bonhomme township, as now established; thence north with the eastern boundary of said township to the Missouri river. So much of said county as lies north and east of said line shall constitute district number one, and so much of said county as lies south and west of said line shall constitute number two. One justice of the county court shall be elected by the qualified voters of each of said districts, and the presiding justice of said county court shall be elected at large by the qualified voters of said county. Said county shall be divided and numbered in the same manner into two representative districts, and until otherwise districted by law, one representative in the general assembly of the state shall be elected by the qualified voters of each of said districts. Immediately succeeding the election in November, 1876, and when the result thereof is officially determinated as hereinafter provided, the justices of the county court shall meet at James C. Sutton's house, on the Manchester road, for the purpose of organizing the new government of the county, determining the bonds of the county officers, and making such appointments as may be authorized by law. Said court may determine at what place in said county said court shall meet and the county offices be located until the question of a permanent seat of justice may be determined. . . .

THE CIVIC LEAGUE OF ST. LOUIS, 1909

The Civic League, which was formed as a means of reforming the political situation of the city, had accomplished a great deal by 1909, when this pamphlet was issued. It had worked to improve living, working, sanitary, recreational and other aspects of municipal life.

(Source: Civic League of St. Louis. What the League Is. What the League Has Done. Officers. . . . St. Louis, 1909.)

What the League Is

The Civic League of St. Louis is an independent non-partisan association designed to unite the efforts of all citizens who are seeking to improve municipal conditions in this city.

Its General Purposes Are:
  To labor for the enactment and strict enforcement of laws.
  To create public sentiment in favor of better municipal conditions and to crystallize that sentiment into action.
  To serve as a bureau of civic information to the citizens.
  To support every movement which will make St. Louis a more healthful, comfortable, attractive city.

Its Policy Is:
  To take no action and make no recommendations until full and careful investigation has been made.
  To confine its activities to the improvement of physical conditions and the general appearance of the City.
  To work with, rather than in opposition to city officials.
  To do constructive work.

What the League Has Done

  Playgrounds Collected and spent $15,000.00 in maintaining playgrounds in the crowded districts. When their usefulness was proven the City was induced to take charge of them. The City now maintains eight public playgrounds.
  Public Baths Conducted free shower baths at the League playgrounds until the city made provisions for free public baths. The city now maintains two public baths.

<u>Vacation Schools</u> Established and maintained for two summers vacations schools. The Board of Education was convinced of their value and took charge of them. The Board now maintains three vacation schools.

<u>School Gardens</u> Maintained gardens for five hundred boys and girls until they were taken over by the Public Recreation Commission.

<u>Tree Planting</u> Drafted and secured the passage of the ordinance creating the office of City Forester. Tree planting has increased fifty per cent since the appointment of the City Forester.

<u>Street Lighting</u> Made an investigation and published an illustrated report on "Street Lighting in St. Louis." Organized the Down Town Lighting Association which has secured an up-to-date lighting system for the business districts.

<u>A New Charter</u> Four years ago began campaign for new city charter. Organized the Joint Charter Conference. . .

<u>Housing</u> Investigated tenement houses in crowded sections, published an illustrated report showing unhealthy surroundings, drafted and secured the passage of ordinances to remedy and prevent further bad sanitary and living conditions.

<u>Smoke</u> Investigated fully the smoke nuisance, published a report showing conditions and planned and urged the passage of a new ordinance for the reorganization of the Smoke Department.

<u>Centennial</u> Organized the movement which resulted in making the Centennial Celebration an official event, which insured its success.

* * *

<u>Streets</u> Is working toward passage of ordinances to improve the appearance of the streets by removal of wires and poles, billboards, and other unnecessary obstructions. Is advocating the passage of a more comprehensive street planning ordinance.

<u>Parks and Boulevards</u> Secured the appointment in 1903 of the Kingshighway Commission and the favorable vote of $500,000 appropriation for the Boulevard, $672,000 appropriation for the small parks, and $700,000 for the purchase of the Old Fair Grounds. Also secured the passage of a bill enabling the city and county to establish an outer park system, which will be voted on in 1910.

<u>City Plan</u> Compiled and published an illustrated book "A City Plan for St. Louis," containing plans for public building group, parks and boulevards, river front, street improvements and, in general, a more artistic treatment of public works. Is actively enegaged in securing the adoption of these recommendations.

<u>Municipal Information</u> Is supplying citizens and officials with speakers on municipal subjects; is collecting reports and building up a municipal library; is keeping a record of all legislation affecting the city; and is actively urging the adoption and the enforcement of up-to-date ordinances which will make the city cleaner, more healthful and more attractive.

NEW CITY CHARTER, JUNE 30, 1914

The citizens of St. Louis adopted a new charter including many of the reform proposals of the progressive era. The initiative, referendum and recall were developed as part of the government and political life of the city. The selections printed below indicate the new aspects of the charter.

(Source: Charter of the City of St. Louis, Missouri. Adopted by Vote of the People, June 30, 1914. In effect from August 29, 1914.)

ARTICLE III.

Recall.

Section 1. Any Elective officer may be recalled by the voters of the City, or if he shall have been elected by the voters of a ward or district, then by the voters of such ward or District, as hereinafter provided.

Sec. 2. A Petition for such recall shall be signed by registered voters equal in number to twenty per cent of all the registered voters of the City at the time of the last preceding regular mayoralty election; provided that in such number shall be included twenty per cent of the registered voters at said time in each of at least two-thirds of the wards of the City; provided further that if the officer shall have been elected by voters of a ward or district, the petition need be signed by only twenty per cent of all the registered voters therein at the time of said mayoralty election

Sec. 3. The signatures need not all be appended to one paper, but all papers comprising the petition shall be uniform in character and shall each be verified by affidavit stating that each signature thereto was made in affiant's presence by, as affiant verily believes, the person whose name it purports to be. Each signer shall state, opposite his signature, his residence address. Any person shall be deemed a registered voter whose name is unerased on the registration books.

Sec. 4. Each of the papers comprising the petition shall state the name and office of the officer whose recall is sought and ask for his recall before any signature is appended thereto.

Sec. 5. All papers comprising the petition shall be assembled by the petitioners and filed with the Board of Election Commissioners as one instrument, and within ten days thereafter said Board shall find and certify as to the sufficiency of the petition, stating the number of registered voters signing. If the petition is certified to be insufficiently signed, supplemental papers conforming to the requirements for the originals may be filed within twenty days thereafter, and said Board, within ten days after such supplements are filed, shall find and certify as to the sufficiency of the petition, so supplemented. If found still insufficiently signed, no further supplement shall be allowed, but a new petition may be filed.

Sec. 6. If such recall petition, with supplements, if any, be found sufficient, a certificate to that effect shall be mailed by said Board to the officer, and if he does not resign within ten days after such mailing, said Board shall provide for submitting the question of his recall at the first election, at which it may lawfully be submitted, not less than thirty nor more than ninety days after such mailing, and if there is no such election, then at a special election to be held within such ninety days if legally possible, otherwise at the earliest day at which said question may be submitted at either a general or special election. Any such election, at any stage thereof, shall at once be discontinued upon the death, resignation or removal of the officer whose recall is in question.

Sec. 7. The ballot shall state the proposition, "Shall (name of officer) be removed from the office of (name of office)?" and to the right thereof, in bold type, the words "yes" and "no," one above the other. To vote for the recall of said officer the voter shall strike out the word "no," and to vote against such recall, the word "yes." If the majority of the votes cast thereon at said election shall be in favor of such recall, the office shall be vacant five days thereafter.

Sec. 8. No petition shall seek the recall of more than one officer, but several propositions for recall may be separately submitted at the same election on the same ballot.

Sec. 9. No recall petition shall be filed against any officer within the first six months or the last six months of his term nor within six months after a proposition for his recall has been defeated at an election.

* * *

ARTICLE V.

The Initiative.

Section 1. The people shall have power, at their option, to propose ordinances, including ordinances proposing amendments to this Charter, and to adopt the same at the polls, with the same effect as if adopted by the Board of Aldermen and approved by the Mayor, such power being known as the Initiative. It shall be exercised as hereinafter provided, subject to the provisions of this Charter.

Sec. 2. Such an ordinance shall be proposed by petition signed by registered voters equal in number to five per cent, or, in case the proposed ordinance is for the submission of an amendment to the Charter, ten per cent of all the registered voters of the City at the time of the last preceding regular mayorality election. Each of the papers comprising the petition shall contain the proposed ordinance in full and designate by names and addresses five persons as the committee of the petitioners.

Sec. 3. Each such petition and the papers comprising same shall be governed by, and proceedings shall be had thereon in accordance with, the provisions of Sections 3 and 5 of Article III concerning the Recall, but construing said sections with reference to the petition and the sufficiency thereof required by this article.

Sec. 4. If the Board of Election Commissioners find that the petition, with supplements, if any, is sufficient, it shall forthwith certify that fact, together with a copy of the petition, omitting signatures, to the Board of Aldermen. Unless the proposed ordinance is, without amendment, adopted and approved by the Mayor, or adopted, without amendment, over his veto, within sixty days after the regular meeting of the Board of Aldermen next after said certification, or unless four members of the committee of the petitioners shall, within fifteen days after the expiration of said sixty days, state in writing to the Clerk of the Board of Aldermen that there is no necessity for submitting the proposed ordinance to the voters, said Clerk shall forthwith certify the failure to adopt same to the Board of Election Commissioners. Said Board of Election Commissioners shall there upon provide for submitting said proposed ordinance, in its original form, to the voters at the first election, at which such submission may lawfully be had, not less than thirty days after such certification to it by said Clerk, and if there is no such election within ninety days after such certification, and the petition shall be signed by registered voters equal in number to seven per cent, or in case the proposed ordinance is for the submission of an amendment to the Charter, fifteen per cent, of all the registered voters of the City at the time of the last preceding regular mayoralty election, then such submission shall be at a special election to be held within such ninety days if legally possible, otherwise at the earliest day on which such submission may be had at either a general or special election.

Sec. 5. The ballots shall state the nature of the proposed ordinance, and to the right thereof in bold type the words "yes" and "no", one above the other. To vote for such ordinance the voter shall strike out the word "no" and to vote against it, the word "yes." If a majority voting on the proposed ordinance vote in favor thereof, it shall be an ordinance of the City, in effect ten days thereafter, and the Board of Election Commissioners shall certify a copy thereof and the fact of its adoption to the Register, who shall number said ordinance and file and preserve said copy and certificate in his office. Such ordinance shall be published and printed copies thereof made for distribution as provided for other ordinances.

Sec. 6. No ordinance adopted at the polls under the Initiative shall be amended or repealed by the Board of Aldermen except by vote of two-thirds of all the members, nor within one year after its adoption.

ARTICLE VI.

The Referendum.

Section 1. The people shall have power, at their option, to approve or reject at the polls any ordinance (except it be an emergency measure as defined in Section 20 of Article IV), such power being known as the Referendum and to invoked and exercised as herein provided.

Sec. 2. If within thirty days after the approval by the Mayor of any ordinance (not an emergency measure) or its adoption over his veto, there is filed with the Board of Election Commissioners a petition purporting to be signed by registered voters equal in number to two per cent of all the registered voters of the City at the time of the last preceding regular mayoralty election, requesting that said ordinance be reconsidered and rejected or referred, then said Board shall certify that fact to the Register and said ordinance shall not take effect except as hereinafter provided. Within ten days after such filing the said Board shall find and certify the number of registered voters signing said petition and what percentage said number equals of the entire number of said registered voters at the time of said election. If the percentage so found is less than the two per cent aforesaid, said Board shall certify that fact to the Register, the said petition shall not be supplemented, and said ordinance shall take effect. If the percentage so found is not less than two per cent but is less than seven per cent of all of said registered voters at the time of said election, then within thirty days after the certification of such finding there may be filed with said Board a supplemental petition, shown, by the affidavits appended thereto, to be signed by registered voters to a number which, with the number of registered voters who signed the original petition, equals in number said seven per cent. If such supplemental petition is filed, said Board shall within ten days thereafter find and certify the number of registered voters signing same and whether such signers, added to registered voters who signed the original petition, equal in number said seven per cent. If it finds that the aggregate number of such signers does not equal said seven per cent, or if the committee of the petitioners make the statement in writing as hereinafter mentioned, said Board shall certify the fact to the Register, no further supplementing shall be permitted, and said ordinance shall take effect. If said Board finds the original petition, or the original and supplemental petitions together, to be signed by registered voters equal in number to said seven per cent, it shall, forthwith after either such finding, certify that fact, together with a copy of the petition (omitting the signatures), to the Register and to the Board of Aldermen, and the latter Board shall reconsider said ordinance. If on such reconsideration the Board of Aldermen by a majority vote rejects said ordinance, it shall not take effect. If the Board of Aldermen fails to finally and wholly reject said ordinance within thirty days after such certification to it, then, unless four members of the committee of the petitioners, within fifteen days after said thirty days expire, state in writing to the clerk of the Board of Aldermen that there is no necessity for submitting said ordinance to the voters, such Clerk shall forthwith certify said failure to the Board of Election Commissioners, which shall thereupon make provision for submitting such ordinance, in such form as it then shall be, to the voters; <u>provided</u>, that the final percentage of signers required to compel submission to the voters of an ordinance amending or repealing an ordinance adopted at the polls under the Initiative shall be three per cent instead of seven per cent as required in case of other ordinances. Such submission shall be at the first election, at which it may lawfully be had, not less than thirty days after the last mentioned certification, and if there is no such election within ninety days after such certification, and the original petition or the original and supplemental petitions together shall be signed by registered voters equal in number to twelve per cent of all the registered voters of the City at the time of the aforesaid mayoralty election, or if the Board of Aldermen shall by resolution so request, such submission shall be at a special election to be held within such ninety days if legally possible, otherwise at the earliest day on which such submission may be had at either a general or special election. If the majority of the votes cast thereon at the election shall be for such ordinance, it shall take effect within ten days after such election.

Sec. 3. The provisions of Section 5 of Article V concerning the ballots and manner of voting, the duties of the Board of Election Commissioners and the Register, and the publishing of ordinances and printing of copies thereof, shall govern like matters under this Article.

Sec. 4. The signatures need not all be appended to one paper, but all papers comprising any original or supplemental petition under this Article shall be uniform in character and shall each set forth the ordinance in full and contain the request mentioned in Section 2, and designate by names and addresses five persons as the committee of the petitioners, and each such paper shall be verified by an affidavit stating the number of signatures thereto and that each signature was made in affiant's presence, by, as affiant verily believes, the person whose name it purports to be; and all papers comprising an original or supplemental petition shall be assembled by the petitioners and filed with the Board of Election Commissioners as one instrument. Each signer shall state opposite his signature his residence address. Any person shall be deemed a registered voter within the meaning of this Article whose name is unerased on the registration books.

Sec. 5. If the provisions of two or more initiated or referred ordinances adopted or approved at the same election conflict, the one receiving the highest affirmative vote shall prevail in so far as such provisions conflict.

* * *

SEGREGATION ORDINANCE, MARCH 3, 1916

The St. Louis government passed this segregation ordinance requiring that blacks and whites live on separate blocks. In addition, churches, schools and other buildings had to be used in segregated fashion. All building permits were to be issued only after specific statements had been made as to whether buildings were to be occupied by white or colored persons.

(Source: Revised Code of St. Louis 1926 . . . St. Louis, 1928.)

ARTICLE XXI

Segregation

Sec. 3819. Who prohibited. -- That, from and after the passage of this ordinance, it shall be unlawful for any white person to use as a residence, or place of abode, any house, building, or structure, or any part thereof, located in any colored block, as the same is hereinafter defined, and it shall also be unlawful for any colored person to use as a residence or place of abode, any residence or place of abode, any house, building, or structure, or any part thereof, located in any white block as the same is hereinafter defined. Provided, however, that nothing herein contained shall preclude persons of either race employed as servants by persons of the other race from residing upon the premises on which they are so employed, and that nothing herein contained shall be construed or operate to prevent any person who, at the date of the passage of this ordinance, shall have acquired a legal right to occupy as a residence, any building or portion thereof, from exercising such legal right, and that nothing in this ordinance contained shall be construed to apply to the use of any building or structure, except such as are, or hereafter may be, located within either a white or a colored block, as hereinbefore defined.

Sec. 3820. Block-meaning -- . . . "White block." A white block shall be construed to mean a block, as hereinabove defined, which was such at the date of the passage of this ordinance, or which at any time hereafter shall become a block, in which white persons are residing and in which no colored persons are residing, except such, if any, as may be employed as servants by white residents therein, as provided in section 3819 hereof; also any block which may hereafter be formed, in which at the date of the passage of this ordinance, there were no residents, or which at any time hereafter may become a block in which white persons are residing and in which no colored persons are residing, except such, if any, as may be employed as servants by white residents therein, as provided by section 3819 hereof.

"Colored block." A colored block shall be construed to mean a block as hereinabove defined, which at the time of the passage of this ordinance, or since, shall have become or which shall hereafter become a block in which colored persons are residing, and in which no white persons are residing, except such, if any, as may be employed as servants by colored residents therein, as provided in section 3819 hereof; also any block as the same is hereinabove defined, heretofore formed, or any block which may be hereafter formed, in which at the date of the passage of this ordinance there were no residents, but which since the passage of this ordinance shall have become or which at any time hereafter may become a block in which colored persons are residing, and in which no white persons are residing, except such, if any, as may be employed as servants by colored residents therein, as provided by section 3819.

* * *

BUILDINGS USED AS CHURCHES, SCHOOLS, ETC.

Sec. 3821. Buildings used as churches, etc. -- That after the passage of this ordinance, no buildings or portion of any building, in the city of St. Louis, shall be used as a church or for the purpose of conducting religious services, or for a school, a theater, a dance hall, or assemblage hall, by white people in a colored block, as the same is hereinabove defined, and after the passage of this ordinance, no building or portion of a building in the city of St. Louis, shall be used as a church or for the purpose of conducting therein religious services, or for a school, a theater, a dance hall, or an assemblage hall, by colored people in a white block, as the same is defined in this ordinance; provided, however, that nothing herein contained shall apply to any building or portion of a building which at the time of the passage of this ordinance is being used as a church or for the purpose of conducting religious services, or for a school, a theater, a dance hall or an assemblage hall, or which at the time of the passage of this ordinance any person or persons or corporation shall have acquired the legal right to use as a church or place for conducting religious services, as a school, a theater, a dance hall, or an assemblage hall.

* * *

POST-WORLD WAR I PLANNING, 1918

The City of St. Louis recognized the necessity for improvement of its facilities. Taking advantage of the lessons learned during the war, the City Plan Commssion indicated that the nations' railroads had been proven insufficient for carrying the industrial products of the country. Inland waterways would have to provide additional freight carriage, and St. Louis could take advantage of the situation to improve its commercial and industrial position. This would raise the economic status of the city and its citizens. The introduction to the report indicating the hopes and aspirations of the people follows.

(Source: Saint Louis, Missouri. The City Plan Commission. St. Louis After the War. St. Louis, 1918.)

ST. LOUIS AFTER THE WAR

It being a function of the City Plan Commission, as provided by ordinance, to make such recommendations as will "tend to make St. Louis a greater city," the following facts and conclusions respecting future public work in St. Louis have been prepared for consideration at a time when no city which claims or aspires to greatness can afford to ignore its responsibilities. The burden of "reconstruction," the term we now choose to describe the period following the close of the war, will fall largely upon the cities -- the centers of commerce and industry. What is St. Louis' responsibility in the reconstruction program?

St. Louis' Responsibility in the Reconstruction Period

In accordance with the executive order issued by the President of the United States on May 11, 1918, the National Research Council, through its committee on reconstruction, is making a study of after-war or reconstruction problems. This committee has defined "reconstruction" as "the rebuilding on normal peace lines of the activities, mental and physical, with such improvement or advance in ideals, methods and machinery as may have been made possible by recent experience. It begins primarily with the returning soldier, in his rehabilitation if necessary, and his return to the industry which best suits his capacities and desires. It includes the placing of other war workers as conditions change and of any human effort where it may be most effective. It means better use of our natural resources in lands, minerals, waters and forests, to furnish larger and more nearly equal opportunities for each citizen and the placing of industry, including agriculture, mining and transportation, on a bsis to meet the changed needs of the country. In short, it means the intelligent planning and execution of plans for a better community. The scope of research is defined as research for reconstruction which should touch upon all lines of science and especially their application to the public welfare."

St. Louis, then, should plan and EXECUTE plans for the betterment of the community. But what kind of plans shall they be? Certainly, we would not wish to execute plans for the mere pleasure of expending money or which will not of themselves produce a return in money or in conservation or preservation of life. The above definition of reconstruction gives the answer quite clearly. Could anything be more distinctly a "better use of our natural resources in . . . waters" than the development of our riverfront for industrial and transportation purposes, for instance? Could anything be more in the interest of public welfare than the building of much needed sewers and a new waterworks, when conditions justify their construction? Or, taking the rehabilitation of the returning soldier as a first essential and assuming a temporary period of industrial inactivity, which is at least possible, would not the execution of the River des Peres Plan furnish welcome temporary employment to hundreds if not thousands of returning soldiers already experienced in large works of this nature involving the building of bridges, railroads, sewers, grading, excavating, etc.? Certainly these are logical conclusions. Other cities are beginning to reach similar conclusions. But, to postpone for the moment, consideration of specific plans, let us consider the position of St. Louis with respect to other large cities, to the nation at large and its ability to undertake large public works.

The Opportunity of St. Louis

Previous to the Civil War, St. Louis was the metropolis of the Central West. It was the leading railroad center as well as the largest city in point of population and manufactures west of the Allegheny Mountains. Being virtually on the boundary line between North and South, and itself the scene of numerous outbreaks, the four years of comparative inactivity from 1861-1865 were sufficient to divert the channels of industry and traffic elsewhere and Chicago assumed a lead which St. Louis has never since been able to overcome. With the outbreak of the European War in 1914 industrial conditions in the United States were considerably affected and continuously so until 1917, when this country entered the war, when industrial conditions underwent the greatest revolution they have ever experienced. Disregarding the reasons, it is a well known fact that the great majority of war industries are located along or adjacent to the Atlantic seaboard. For various reasons the federal government has recently seen fit to attempt a decentralization at least so far as new industries are concerned, but St. Louis and other mid-western cities have not secured anything like the proportion existing in the eastern cities. St. Louis and other cities of the middle west have seen their ranks of industrial workers and business men somewhat depleted because of the demand for men in the shipyards and war industries of the east. In this temporary realignment of industry some have seen, or professed to see, a further detriment to the future development of St. Louis, industrial and otherwise. But is this actually the case?

Our war industries have been more or less of a mushroom character. Unlike Germany, we have never conceived an industrialism based on the demands of war, nor do we now. It is questionable, therefore, how much of permanent benefit will accrue to eastern cities as a result of the war industries. Their very presence in some cases, will prove to be a serious after-the-war problem. Few eastern cities have had the foresight or the time to so plan for their war industrial expansion as to make of it a decided factor in the future development of those cities.

On the other hand, the war has brought out conclusively the inadequacy of eastern terminals to handle the output of the nation and certainly this nation is still more or less in its infancy from a production standpoint. The war, too, has emphasized the absurdity of our previous faith in railroads to handle economically all forms of traffic. Inland waterway development has become an economic as well as a physical necessity, and we may safely anticipate it on very nearly as great a scale as the development of the railroads in the last half of the nineteenth century. The rivers of Europe are used as extensively as the railroads. For obvious reasons America must do likewise following the war. In this respect probably no city has greater opportunities than St. Louis, particularly if the opportunity is seized in time. . . .

Industry is one of the prime requisites of modern civilization. America owes much of its present greatness to the master minds that have here developed many of the improved methods of industrial efficiency. The stress of the war has produced still greater advances in the science of industry. In the period of reconstruction which follows the war, science will play a greater part than ever before in the advancement of industry. One result which should inevitably follow is the stimulation of manufacturing products near the centers of production of raw materials. St. Louis, being nearer perhaps than other large cities to many of the great production centers of raw materials of the country, should, if wisely directed, become an ever greater center of manufacture and of industry. In the manufacture of cotton and woolen goods, tobacco, agricultural implements and as a grain and live stock market, St. Louis has hardly begun to attain the growth its geographical position warrants.

St. Louis now possesses a terminal system reputed to be the best in the United States, if not in the world. With the completion of the Municipal Railroad Terminal system and additional river terminals there will be unlimited opportunity for industrial expansion.

Not the least of the lessons that America is learning from the war is the importance of a high standard of living for all classes of men. Good homes and good living conditions are absolutely essential to industrial efficiency and as much to be desired as large financial returns, if not infinitely more so. First at the shipyards and now near war industrial plants throughout the country, the federal government has seen fit and necessary to provide houses for workmen and their families of a standard far better than anything ever attempted in this country before. European nations have long realized and attempted to meet this condition, and they are contemplating expenditures of billions of dollars on housing after the war. . . .

CENTRAL RIVER FRONT PLAN, 1928

As part of the city's development program, reconstruction of the river front area was recognized as an important element for the maintenance and improvement of St. Louis' commercial and industrial position. The plan recommended additional roadway as well as creation of a river front plaza.

(Source: St. Louis. City Plan Commission. A Plan for the Central River Front. St. Louis, Missouri, 1928.)

The Plan

The plan proposed in this report is composed of a number of interdependent projects. Each is necessary for the fulfillment of the entire plan and to secure the full benefits to be derived from it. . . . For purposes of brevity they are here summarized as follows:

1. A new thoroughfare 100 feet wide from the north and northwestern part of the City to Third Street in the business district.

2. A new thoroughfare 100 feet wide from the south and southwestern part of the City to Third Street in the business district.

3. Construction of elevated roadways in these two thoroughfares having capacity for six lines of high-speed, non-stop traffic.

4. Widening and double-decking of Third Street (140 feet wide) from Poplar Street to Morgan Street.

5. Acquisition of all the property between Third Street and the river from Spruce Street to Franklin Avenue for a riverfront plaza.

6. Construction of a high level mall between Market and Chestnut Streets from the Old Court House to the river, with extensions along the riverfront. . .

7. Use of lower levels of Riverfront Plaza for parking space and garage, subway terminals, and the like.

8. Direct connection between Third Street high level roadway and upper deck of the Municipal Bridge.

9. Widening of the Locust, Olive, Pine and Walnut Streets between Third and Fourth Streets to provide direct access between the business district and the upper level of widened Third Street.

Some of the numerous benefits and advantages to be accomplished by this plan may be briefly summarized as follows:

1. Shifting of the business district will be permanently checked.

2. Property values of the eastern end of the business district will be stabilized and greatly enhanced.

3. The greatly increased street capacity will be a decided advantage to traffic circulation facilities throughout the City, since the plan is completely co-ordinated with the Major Street Plan.

4. The long sought improvement of the river front will be accomplished in a most monumental manner.

5. Demand for public parking space and garage facilities upon a large scale will be satisfied, since the plan provides an ultimate capacity for the accomodation of more than 8,000 automobiles.

6. Both vehicular and water approach to the City of St. Louis will be highly attractive and exciting.

* * *

PLANS FOR ST. LOUIS AFTER WORLD WAR II,
December, 1942

During the Second World War the city government already recognized the necessity of postwar planning. Taking as a basis the idea that the city had a place in the future development of the nation, the planning commission proceeded to make recommendations which if followed would help in the rehabilitation and improvement of the city. The selection from the report printed below indicates that the commission recognized the necessity of covering the urban area as a whole, and recommended that plans be developed for the land as a whole.

(Source: St. Louis, Missouri. City Plan Commission. Saint Louis After World War II. St. Louis, December, 1942.)

Chapter III. A REALISTIC LAND PROGRAM

In an era of expanding economy the creation of new values may be sufficiently large to obscure certain losses incident to the process of growth. In an era of more stable economy when few new values are created it is imperative that losses be prevented. Conservation of all existing values must be the controlling policy.

St. Louis is confronted with a condition of unprecedented magnitude. To deal with it effectively necessitates profound changes in the traditional methods and policies that have heretofore characterized urban development. Compromises and halfway measures will neither solve the problem nor ameliorate the difficulty. There must be broad vision, and policy and firm enforcement of the measures and controls directed, and enforcement characterized not by momentary vigor and enthusiasm but by sustained application over a long period of years.

... Broadly speaking, the policy required. . . is:

Obsolete Areas must be reconstructed by large scale methods.

Blighted Districts must be rehabilitated and given sounder protection.

Newly Developed Areas must be stabilized and given sounder protection.

Before considering controls and measures involved in implementing these policies let us examine two broad underlying conditions: (1) Is St. Louis' future position in the national economic structure such as to justify extensive rehabilitation and reconstruction? (2) What local practices had led to present conditions and to what extent will any of these handicap a broad program of rehabilitation and reconstruction?

(1) There is no sound reason why St. Louis should become decadent. This City has always ranked well up among the ten largest American cities. Its strategic location, its favorable transportation facilities, the character and diversification of its industries, its wholesale and retail trade and other factors all demonstrate its basic economic strength. Extensive research would reveal no good reason why St. Louis should not continue to play a most significant part in the future development of the nation. Its many natural advantages should enable it to keep in the forefront of large American cities even though local citizens and their leaders fail to make the most of these advantages. Complacency is St. Louis' greatest deficiency.

(2) The second question is not as easily answered. Our basic local difficulty stems from the lack of unification and control of the process of urbanization. St. Louis is separate from St. Louis County. In the latter over 300,000 persons now reside. . . . Much urbanization is taking place outside the incorporated areas in St. Louis County. Urban expansion has far outrun the limits of economic justification or of social need.

It has been suggested that since so much new wealth and development occurs in suburban areas beyond the City limits, the consolidation of the whole urban area into a single uniform municipality would remedy the situation by offsetting the losses in the central city with the new values created in the suburbs. There is no question but that the sharp political division between City and County is unfortunate. Physically and economically there is but one city. . .

Unification of the entire urban area would not per se constitute a sound solution of problems heretofore described. It would have to be supplemented by wholly new measures to limit unnecessary economic expansion. There would be a distinct gain in so doing, an immense advantage now lost in the haphazard process of uncontrolled expansion. There would be a further gain in reduction of the total cost of government. . . .

The problem with which we are here concerned therefore, urban obsolescence and blight, is mainly a matter of keeping all types of our residential structures in good condition. We have tolerated neglect and decadence because of overemphasis of new suburban growth. We failed to appraise the true cost of such unbalanced development. We refused to acknowledge symptoms of a deep-seated malady and to examine its cause and portent. We closed our eyes and tried to ignore the warnings. We said that we had to have cheap land where the City could expand and grow. Speculative builders and landowners continued to capitalize on this false assumption that it was cheaper to build on less expensive suburban land. This assumption is erroneous for two reasons; (1) Only the initial costs are low in suburban areas and these increase gradually as full improvements and municipal services are provided until, eventually, they equal or surpass said costs in the central city; and (2) because we have failed to explore the possibilities and benefits of large scale reconstruction of central areas. . . .

Our problems of blight and obsolescence are not due entirely to unfortunate local conditions and practices. Whether or not we achieve unification of the entire area of our urbanization there is need of new policies and measures heretofore lacking in past practices of municipal growth. We can no longer ignore the decadent areas of St. Louis. It is apparent that these areas must be reconditioned and rebuilt. . . .

DOCUMENTS 113

PLAN FOR PUBLIC RECREATION AREAS, 1944

In addition to proper school facilities, the need
for recreational areas is essential in total city
and residential planning. The City Plan Commission investigated the needs of each age group
and recommended the addition of facilities in
all areas of the city. These included parks,
playgrounds and community centers. The plans
were specifically developed so that the City
could follow a long-range program.

(Source: Saint Louis, Missouri. City Plan Commission. <u>Plan for Public
Recreational Areas</u>. St. Louis, Missouri, 1944.)

I. PRINCIPLES OF A COMPREHENSIVE RECREATION SYSTEM.

A comprehensive system of recreational facilities must serve all sections of the City and must be so diversified as to supply the needs of all age groups.

Pre-School Children Need Adequate Home Grounds

Small children below school age must be under constant parental observation and their play needs can best be met in and around the home. In the overcrowded apartment house areas where such open space is not available, interior block playgrounds should be provided by cooperation of the property owners. The provision of fresh air and space for protected play for preschool children in primarily the responsibility of the parents. Zoning and building regulations will be helpful in preventing future overcrowding of land.

Elementary School Children Need Playgrounds for Supervised Play Activities

Children of elementary school age are under the direction of educational authorities a considerable part of the time. Recreation is now an integral part of the school curriculum and the school playground is intensively used during school hours. Each elementary school should be located on a site large enough to provide supervised play on an all-year basis. Supervised playgrounds at the elementary schools can be made usable at all times; they will be within walking distance of all of the children and duplication of facilities will be avoided.

Youths of High School Age Need Areas for Active Sports

Boys and girls of this age are interested in all forms of athletics and active sports which require larger areas than the playgrounds. The logical location for play or athletic fields is at the High Schools, and in addition to the school play fields, provisions should be made for similar facilities in the public parks. These can be used by youths not in school and by older persons. The Board of Education and the Park Department are thus jointly responsible for acquiring and developing this type of recreational area.

Adults Need Areas for Both Passive and Active Recreation

Adults are generally more interested in quiet, passive recreation than in organized and competitive athletics. For them there should be neighborhood parks, large parks, pleasure drives, small ornamental areas and community centers for indoor recreation. Adults who prefer outdoor tennis, baseball and similar activites may use the play fields. Park Officials are primarily responsible for providing recreational facilities for adults.

There is, of course, an intermingling of age uses in the various types of recreational areas. All persons use the larger parks and adults use the play fields. The above described facilities will, however, meet the dominant recreational needs of all persons within the urban area. . . .

SUMMARY

A comparison of the existing recreational areas in St. Louis with accepted modern standards for such areas reveals that:

1. The total park area should be increased by one hundred sixty-five percent.
2. At least thirty more neighborhood parks with a minimum area of twenty acres each are needed.
3. The area now devoted to play fields should be quadrupled.
4. The area now devoted to playgrounds is one-third of what it should be.
5. Seventy percent of the city's residential neighborhoods need community centers.

The city's inadequate provision for recreational needs is very great. The situation must be corrected before the city can become a good place in which to live -- before stable and attractive residential neighborhoods can be developed and maintained. - - -

COMPREHENSIVE CITY PLAN, 1947

The City government recognized the necessity of becoming involved in a program of rehabilitation of various "blighted" areas of St. Louis. Although the war could be partly blamed for this action, the areas had been neglected for a long period of time. Recommendations were made for improvement of units to provide better light and sanitary conditions as well as maintenance. The planning commission insisted that the proposals made had to be carried out, and that the Model City Planning Enabling Act should be enacted.

(Source: St. Louis. City Plan Commission. Comprehensive City Plan. Saint Louis, Missouri, 1947.)

BLIGHTED DISTRICTS

The most important single requisite for the improvement of housing in St. Louis is the enactment of a Minimum Standards Housing Ordinance. The City Plan Commission, the Building Commissioner and the Health Department with the aid and assistance of the American Public Health Association, have collaborated in the preparation of such an ordinance which provides for:

1. Elimination of overcrowding by prescribed minimum standards of space per family and per person.
2. The number, area, and openability of windows permitting entrance of fresh air and natural light.
3. Screens on doors and windows to restrict flies or mosquitoes.
4. Elimination of basement rooms as dwelling units unless they comply with the provisions set forth in the ordinance.
5. Improvement of sanitary conditions by elimination of hopper water closets and privies in sewered areas within six years of effective date of ordinance.
6. The location of water closets and the number of persons using them.
7. Keeping dwelling units in a clean, sanitary, habitable condition and free from infestation.
8. Maintenance and repair of dwellings necessary to provide tightness to the weather and reasonable possibilities of heating.
9. Installation of flues which would permit the operation of heating equipment to maintain adequate temperature in each habitable room.
10. Adequate daylight or fixtures for artificial illumination in public halls, bathrooms and other habitable rooms.

<u>Unless and until such an ordinance has been adopted and enforced, most housing areas in St. Louis will continue to deteriorate and blighted districts and obsolete areas will reach much greater proportions</u> than at present.

The rehabilitation of blighted areas is the No Man's Land of housing. It is more important than reconstruction of obsolete areas. It is a field that has been completely neglected partly because it is less spectacular than large scale reconstruction, and partly because the opportunities for profitable investment are presumably less than in a new development. Without a definite plan for the rehabilitation of the present blighted areas new obsolete areas will develop faster than present areas can be reconstructed. . . .

CARRYING OUT THE COMPREHENSIVE PLAN IS OF NO VALUE UNLESS IT IS FOLLOWED.

It is frequently said that American cities, like Topsy, "just grew." Shortly after the year 1900, after a century of planless growth, citizen groups in several cities caused "City Plans" to be prepared and published. . . .

These early city plans had no official status and were not accepted and used by city officials. Only when aggressively sponsored by citizen groups were any of the improvements suggested in these plans carried out. There was no systematic attempt to direct the entire development of the city or to follow a complete city plan.

Because of this state of affairs, and because of the imperative need for preventing haphazard decisions and chaotic conditions in our rapidly growing cities, a second attempt at planning was undertaken by many cities. This consisted of appointing an official city plan commission charged with the responsibility of preparing a comprehensive city plan. It was assumed that the creation of an official plan commission by an ordinance duly enacted by the city council would result in introduction of an official city plan, and that this plan would automatically be accepted and followed. . . .

This second attempt to bring about well planned cities met with only indifferent success in most instances. Many of the commissions failed to prepare a complete plan either because of inadequate knowledge and understanding of the work involved or because they were not given funds to carry out their task. A few did manage to secure funds and to prepare a plan but soon found that changing city administrations or indifferent or hostile officials would not accept and follow the plan. There was no means of enforcement. In a few cities, among which St. Louis has been an outstanding leader, plans were prepared and accepted and city officials carried them out over a long period of years with close fidelity. In these cities, however, there is no means of enforcement where the city council or an official in responsible charge of public works chooses to ignore the plan. . . .

To overcome the flaws in this second attempt for effective city plans a third procedure was devised after much study and consideration by the distinguished group of citizens, attorneys, municipal officials and technicians appointed to a nationwide committee. This group produced a model "Standard City Planning Enabling Act." This act provides as follows:

1. "Municipalities are authorized and empowered to make, adopt, amend, extend, add to or carry out a municipal plan and to create by ordinance a planning commission."

2. "For the appointment of a commission comprised partly of public officials and partly of citizens, the latter being in a majority of approximately 2 to 1; such members to serve without compensation."

3. "The city plan commission is empowered to elect a chairman from among the citizen members, shall hold at least one regular meeting each month, shall adopt rules for transaction of business, employ a staff and make expenditures for the conduct of its work within amounts appropriated by the city council."

4. "It shall be the function and duty of the commission to make and adopt a 'master plan' for the physical development of the municipality . . . showing the commission's recommendations for . . . among other things, the general location, character and extent of streets, viaducts, subways, bridges, waterways, water fronts, boulevards, parkways, playgrounds, and open spaces, the general location of public buildings and other public property, and the general location and extent of public utilities and terminals, whether publicly or privately owned or operated, for water, light, sanitation, transportation, communication, power, and other purposes, also the removal, relocation, widening, narrowing, vacating, abandonment, change of use or extension of any of the foregoing ways, grounds, open spaces, buildings, property, utilities, or terminals; as well as a zoning plan for the control of the height, area, bulk, location and use of buildings and premises." . . .

* * *

The purpose of this Act was to require public officials to give careful consideration to officially adopted city plans and to establish a systematic procedure whereby an official city plan would have to be considered before any official action could be taken on any matter affecting the plan. One most significant matter is that the plan is adopted by the plan commission and not by the city council, it having been the conclusion of the committee that adoption by ordinance would "freeze" the plan. By having the city plan commission adopt the plan as a general guide rather than to be officially adopted as a fixed and arbitrary legal instrument, it would be possible to keep the plan flexible and dynamic and to meet changing conditions without the necessity of passing various amendatory ordinances for minute changes of detail.

* * *

ST. LOUIS, 1951

The St. Louis Chamber of Commerce published its view of the city and its environs in 1951. It is a concise picture of the city and its prospects for industry and commerce. In addition a good description of the zoo is presented. It is aimed at prospective tourists, as well as various businesses.

(Source: St. Louis Chamber of Commerce. <u>St. Louis as It Is</u> Today. Issued by the St. Louis Chamber of Commerce and "Visit St. Louis" Committee. St. Louis, 1951.)

ST. LOUIS AS IT IS TODAY

A Modern City rich though it is in historic lore, St. Louis, now a solid and substantial metropolis, is of even greater interest today as a modern American City, full of the vigor of the West. Few can equal it in attractiveness, or as a place in which to live and work and play. . . .

The foremost city of the Mississippi Valley, and the largest between the Great Lakes and the Pacific Coast, St. Louis offers the advantages of modern metropolitan life, with all its exhilarating stir and sparkle. Its immediate urban population is 905,000 but in Metropolitan St. Louis, including its natural suburbs, are more than a million and a half people. Unlike many cities, St. Louis has never known extreme boom periods, for its growth has been sure and steady from the beginning. Thus, its industries, too, have steadily grown, and its people have generally prospered. Its diversified business interests are the best possible guarantee of continued prosperity, and of steady employment for its workers.

Rising westerly from the riverfront, St. Louis and its environs stand on rolling ground, high above water levels. The main business and shopping sections center in an area near the river, with the residential districts spreading like a fan for miles to the north, the west and the south. Continuing along smooth boulevards beyond the City limits are beautiful suburbs containing thousands upon thousands of attractive homes. Farther out among the hills and valleys, are a score of charming country clubs. Just across the river from the downtown heart of the city is East St. Louis, a manufacturing city of some 80,000 people. Other manufacturing sections, segregated from residential areas, are laid out in districts especially favorable for industry. . . .

The Mississippi, with its tugs and steamboats, its barges and tows, its pleasure craft and its ferry boats, all flanked by the Jefferson National Expansion Memorial and the skyscrapers of the nearby business district, forms one of the greatest attractions to visitors. . . .

. . . In the city itself and through its suburbs, streetcar lines and buses cap every section. More than one-half million passengers are carried daily. Especially noticeable to the stranger is the unusually courteous treatment accorded by the St. Louis police. Throughout the city scientific fire protection is afforded by a thoroughly modern system.

From four miles west of the main business section of St. Louis, and forming a center of its own is wonderful Forest Park -- a huge natural playground of nearly 1,400 acres, beautified by artisitc developments of a degree which has made it internationally famous. Surrounding the Park are wide boulevards, lined with splendid residences and magnificent public buildings. Beyond is a great university whose grounds extend for almost a mile along the westward boulevard, and nearby are several preparatory schools. A number of fine residential sections lie immediately to the north, west and south. Many of the parks in different parts of the city, exquisitely cared for, offer rest and recreation in these settings.

To the St. Louis shopping districts come thousands of people from all sections of the country, for the St. Louis shops have a national reputation for style, variety, and value. Nearly all the great manufacturing concerns of America are represented here, St. Louis being recognized as the natural distributing headquarters for a vast consuming population. Hence, practically anything that can be had anywhere is obtainable in its markets.

Because of its location in the center of the country and its superior transportation facilities, St. Louis is the most accessible of American cities. At the cross-roads of the nation, St. Louis sees the ebb and flow of a nation's traffic at its door. Thousands of travelers daily pass through the St. Louis passenger station. Vast, direct trains make it easy to reach almost any of the principal cities of fourteen states by overnight sleeping car without loss of business time. . . .

A splendid network of airlines, radiating out of St. Louis, also makes it possible for the traveler to reach virtually every part of America speedily and comfortably. . . .

THE ST. LOUIS ZOO

. . . Experts concerned with the captivity of live animals come to St. Louis from all parts of this country and abroad to study the ideal methods used here, and particularly to examine the unusual arrangements by which the animal dens and paddocks have been transformed into near-to-nature haunts.

The Zoo occupies 83 acres in Forest Park. Approximately 2,000 living creatures, including mammals, birds, reptiles, and amphibians, have been collected from all parts of the globe to make a balanced representation of the animals of the world. The exhibits are shown in family groups whenever possible, and at all times those species are emphasized which are of great interest to the public.

Unique features of the Zoo are its free animal training performances, given from approximately May 15th to October 12th. . . .

The Zoo has been developed with the plan of showing animals in natural settings, which are not only best for the welfare of the exhibits, but also enable visitors to receive a sense of intimacy with the animals, as if they were observing them in the wild, but safely and at close range. . . .

AVIATION

St. Louis is again becoming the air center of the nation. Long a believer in aviation development and promotion, St. Louis is taking action to gain a provision of preeminence as the American Air Center. By virtue of its geographical and industrial importance alone, St. Louis is destined to be a hub of aviation. Through the efforts of its aviation organizations, St. Louis is moving ahead to help develop air facilities and services required to secure and maintain its rightful place in aviation.

St. Louis is surrounded by a network of thirteen active ariports within a radius of twenty-five miles including a seaplane base, a large airforce base, Lambert-St. Louis Municipal Airport, a metropolitan airport and nine smaller airports. The largest of the airports is Lambert-St. Louis Municipal Airport located conveniently northwest of the City. Lamber Airport is the fastest growing municipal airport in the country. Upon completion of the present expansion program providing for enormous runways, taxi strips and an ultra-modern air terminal, it will be among the finest in the world.

St. Louis is a center of Naval and Military aviation activities. There is a large Naval Air Station which keeps in reserve training over a thousand former navy pilots at Lambert Field. An airforce base located at Scott Field twenty miles east of St. Louis is headquarters for the Air Force Training Command. Headquarters for the Missouri Air National Guard is located on Lambert-St. Louis Municipal Airport.

Air service at St. Louis includes five trunk airlines for mail, passenger, airfreight and an express service to all parts of the world. In addition to the above, there is one cargo carrier and several non-scheduled operations offering passenger and cargo service.

The leading aircraft factory in the area is The McDonnell Aircraft Corporation, manufacturers of the famed Phantom and Banshee first all jet navy fighters and the first jet helicopter. . . .

REPORT OF MAYOR'S TRANSIT OWNERSHIP COMMITTEE, 1952

> After careful consideration of the problems faced by the city because of faltering and increasingly expensive mass transportation as well as greater dependence on the automobile, the mayor's committee recommended that the city take over the mass transit system and operate it. This would also permit local rather than state control, as well as eliminate taxation of the system, which would keep the fares at a reasonable level. The recommendations of the committee indicate the problems involved, and how they could be solved.

(Source: St. Louis. <u>Report of Mayor's Transit Ownership Committee. Findings and Recommendations of Mayor's Transit Ownership Committee.</u> St. Louis, 1952.)

1. Throughout the United States, including the City of St. Louis and its surrounding metropolitan area, there has been a shift from the use of mass transportation facilities to the use of the private automobile as a means of transportation.

2. Contemporaneously with this shift there has been a substantial increase in the cost of operating mass transportation facilities as a result of higher wages and higher prices for materials and supplies.

3. As the result of the decline in the number of riders and the increase in costs the operators of mass transportation facilities have increased fares and curtailed service.

4. The increases in fares and the curtailments in service lead to a further decline in the number of riders, followed by further increases in fare and further curtailment of service.

5. In addition, the increased and constantly increasing use of the automobile as a means of transportation creates in large metropolitan cities serious problems of traffic congestion.

6. Notwithstanding the shift from mass transportation facilities to the private automobile, there are and there will always be in any metropolitan city, including the City of St. Louis, a substantial percentage of the population which is completely dependent upon mass transportation facilities as a means of transportation.

7. An adequate mass transportation system is essential to the preservation of the economic values of any metropolitan city, and this is true of the City of St. Louis.

8. Without such an adequate mass transportation system property val-

ues in the City of St. Louis would inevitably decline, resulting in a loss to the City of substantial revenues derived from the taxation of business property.

9. Private industry in the operation of a mass transportation system is faced and for the forseeable future will probably continue to be faced with the heavy burden of federal income taxes.

10. Private ownership of a mass transportation system is necessarily based upon the making of a reasonable return on the investment.

11. In the State of Missouri such a return allowed by the Public Service Commission of Missouri to other utilities ranges from 6 to 6 1/2 percent. This return is after federal and state income taxes.

12. The next rate base of the St. Louis Public Service Company, as found by the staff of the Missouri Public Service Commission, is approximately $27,000,000.

The net rate base contended for by the Company itself in the case now pending in the Public Service Commission for an increase in fares is approximately $36,800,000.

At the most recent hearing before the Public Service Commission upon application of the St. Louis Public Service Company for an increase in fares, the City of St. Louis contended that the net rate base is less than $27,000,000, and based its contention on a number of reasons, including the following:

(a) That the Company's property account and original cost rate base is burdened with an unproductive and uneconomic investment in 7 remaining street car lines; that this investment is grossly out of proportion to the service provided by such car lines and the operating income theorized from them; that this condition contributes materially to a wide disparity between the real or economic value of the Company's system and its nominal or book value; that during 1951 the Street Railway Lines, which represents 45 per cent of the gross property account and 53 per cent of the net rate base, produced only 29 per cent of passenger revenues, 21 per cent of vehicle miles, 29 per cent of seat miles, and less than 8 per cent of operating income, as reported by the Company.

(b) That straight bus operations would result in a much lesser rate base than the $27,000,000 found by the Commission staff and that the public should not be required to pay higher fares than would be necessary to provide a reasonable return on a straight bus operation.

13. Private industry in mass transportation is subject to state, county, and municipal taxes, which are treated as operating expenses.

14. Subsidies from the City of St. Louis to private owners of a mass transportation system are not permitted under the Constitution and laws of the State of Missouri.

15. When a privately owned transportation system is unable to furnish a reasonable fare, it is the duty of the community as a means for self preservation to provide such service.

16. The concept of public ownership and operation of mass transportation facilities is neither new, revolutionary, nor socialistic.

The present charter of the City of St. Louis, adopted in 1914, contemplated the possibility of public ownership for it contains provisions authorizing the City of St. Louis to own and operate a mass transportation system.

17. A system of public ownership free from political interference or control can be established.

18. A publicly owned system would be freed from the burden of paying federal and state income taxes, and to that extent would have a greater margin for the rendition of adequate service at reasonable fares.

19. A publicly owned system would not be required to earn a profit on the investment, and to that extent would also have a greater margin for the rendition of adequate service at reasonable fares.

20. If the requirements of rendering adequate service at reasonable fares should make it necessary, in the interest of the community as a whole, to subsidize a publicly owned system, such subsidies could legally be granted.

21. In Missouri, the privately owned system operated in the City of St. Louis is subject to regulation by the Public Service Commission of Missouri and the City of St. Louis has no control over the fares or service.

A publicly owned system, created by Charter amendment, would be subject to such local control as would be provided for in such amendment.

Therefore, fares, service and all other aspects of mass transportation would be controlled at a local level.

22. In the absence of a startling and presently unforseeable change in riding habits, privately owned mass transportation systems will find it difficult, if not impossible to attract private capital for expansion and development.

23. The problem of providing adequate mass transportation facilities is inseparable from the traffic problems arising out of the increased, and constantly increasing, use of the private automobile.

A proper balance between use of mass transportation facilities and the use of the private automobile is essential.

24. Mass transportation should be considered as the basic and predominant means of transportation, but the private automobile should have its rightful place as a supplemental vehicle.

25. To achieve a proper balance between the use of mass transportation facilities and the use of the private automobile, in the interest of the community as a whole, a single agency should be established having control of mass transportation facilities and traffic.

26. Such integrated control could be obtained through the creation, by Charter amendment, of a "St. Louis Transit and Traffic Authority."

27. Such Authority should be given supervision, control and management of the publicly owned mass transit system and should be given the power of supervision and control over all aspects of traffic.

28. The Authority would have no power to acquire a transit system unless authority for such acquisition had previously been approved by vote of the people.

29. There should be established a "Mass Transportation Area" which would include those areas in St. Louis County where adequate service at reasonable rates can be furnished without imposing a burden on the system.

30. The St. Louis Transit Authority should be impowered to operate outside the City limits, to enter into contracts for the rendition of service with municipalities in St. Louis County, to enter into contracts with privately or publicly owned transportation systems in St. Louis County, and to merge or consolidate with a St. Louis County Authority or a Metropolitan Authority when conditions justify such merger or consolidation and when the same had been approved by vote of the people.

31. Representation on the Authority could be given to persons who do not reside in the City of St. Louis but who reside in the area served, through the appointment to the Authority of one member who is not a resident of the City of St. Louis but who resides in the area served.

32. Under conditions as they now exist, and are likely to continue for a number of years, the creation of a Metropolitan Transit and Traffic Authority, pursuant to the State Constitution as distinguished from the St. Louis Authority created by amendment to the City Charter is not advisable.

33. The St. Louis Transit and Traffic Authority should be composed of five members appointed by the Board of Estimate and Apportionment. . . .

Not more than three members of the Authority should be of the same political party.

The system should be operated, with the exception of definite and designated key personnel, on a civil service basis, but under civil service rules promulgated by the Authority itself and enforced within the Authority.

In the event the system of the Public Service Company is acquired by the Transit and Traffic Authority, appropriate recognition should be given of the rights of the employees at the time of such acquisition.

34. The Board of Directors of the Public Service Company has advised the Committee that it is neither promoting nor resisting the sale of the transit system to the City.

35. Notwithstanding our recommendation that public ownership under a Transit and Traffic Authority is advisable, the Committee is of the opinion that the City of St. Louis should not undertake to acquire and operate a mass transportation system unless the cost of acquisition, the terms and conditions thereof, and the circumstances existing at the time are such as to make it reasonably certain that the system can be operated on a self-sustaining basis, or without imposition of undue and unfair burdens on the fiscal resources of the City or on the taxpayers. . . .

HOUSING REPORT, AUGUST 1953

The city plan commission had been continuously making studies of the various problems facing St. Louis. Although postwar planning had been carefully developed, funds had not always been made available to carry through all plans. An analysis of housing in certain areas of the city showed that proper maintenance was not being provided in many cases, that facilities were not up to modern standards, and that a lack of sufficient expressways had caused local streets to be overcrowded, leading to deterioration of fashionable neighborhoods. Based on this information the commission developed specific plans for rehabilitation.

(Source: St. Louis City Plan Commission. Division of Building and Division of Health. <u>Let's Look at Housing: A Report on Conditions in Selected Areas of St. Louis.</u> St. Louis, August, 1953.)

THESE ARE THE GENERAL FINDINGS:

1. A large portion of the city needs either reconstruction or rehabilitation of its housing. The reconstruction area covers 22% of the total blocks in the city and 26% of the dwelling units while the rehabilitation area consists of 17% of the city blocks and 27% of the dwelling units. This means that over half of the dwelling units of the city need renovation or reconstruction.
2. It is significant that such areas are contrastingly more widespread in north St. Louis than in south St. Louis.
3. The reconstruction, or slum area, has increased in size considerably since it was first charted by the City Plan Commission in 1942. In 1942 approximately 46,000 dwelling units were in this area. The survey indicates there are now about 67,000 dwelling units in this classification.
4. The general rehabilitation area is smaller than originally charted, comprising approximately 69,000 of the city's 260,000 dwelling units. This is due to the more specific and objective housing quality information made available by the survey. The survey also indicates that in several instances the gradual spread of blight has extended beyond the original boundaries, and in the west end it has reached the city limits opposite University City and Wellston. There is also a small patch of blight opposite Maplewood.

5. There has been a general tendency in older neighborhoods with large homes, to divide these into smaller dwelling units, or to convert to rooming houses causing over-occupancy, crowding, abnormal use of existing utilities and facilities and adding to the parking and traffic problems in the area.
6. The development of haphazard shopping or industrial centers together with attendant minor commercial establishments encroaching on the residential area has had an adverse effect on older neighborhoods, creating among other things, nuisances and new traffic and parking problems.
7. There has been a movement of the large negro population, heretofore concentrated in north-central St. Louis, westward into areas which in the past were entirely occupied by whites. The percentage of the total dwelling units in the city occupied by negroes has increased from 12.5% in 1940 to 15.5% in 1950 according to census data.
8. In general, in neighborhoods, whether old or new, where there is a high proportion of owner-occupied dwellings, the dwelling conditions are better than in those areas which are predominantly tenant occupied. In the areas surveyed approximately 31% of the dwelling units were owner-occupied in south St. Louis while only 26% were owner-occupied in north St. Louis.
9. General lack of repair and maintenance is by far one of the outstanding deficiencies found in the survey, even in some of the better area. Over 50% of the dwelling units surveyed are in need of some major repairs.
10. The lack of adequate toilet and bathing facilities is a major problem in older areas. About 15% of the dwelling units surveyed had no bath available and there are still approximately 9,000 outside toilets existing in the city.
11. Due to the lack of major expressways which could serve as traffic arteries to and from the downtown area, neighborhood streets are being used to carry this traffic load during the morning and evening rush hours. This is especially true in certain parts of the west end where several such streets cut through once fashionable neighborhoods and have caused these neighborhoods to deteriorate very rapidly so that they have become undesirable for normal residential use.
12. Some areas zoned for future industrial expansion contain a considerable amount of existing housing which is in general of poor quality, and these areas should be redeveloped.
13. It appears that some areas bordering on the county and the city limits adjacent to Maplewood, Wellston, and University City are having a blighting effect on both the city and the county. Such fringe areas spread blight in both directions and this indicates that these problem areas should receive the joint consideration of the City and the County.

14. There is a lack of adequate small recreational areas in many sections of the city and this has a bearing on neighborhood housing conditions.
15. The results of the survey show no great problem of overcrowding as measured by present provisions of the Minimum Housing Standards Ordinance which are based on room area. However, the results do indicate that there is serious overcrowding in some areas when measured on the basis of number of persons per room and adequate number of sleeping rooms.
16. There is a correlation between high coverage of the land by structures and accessory buildings and poor housing conditions. In these areas there was higher incidence of daylight obstruction, over-occupancy and many sanitary violations such as accumulation of trash, refuse, garbage, and presence of rats.
17. In areas where there is an intermixture of commercial, industrial, and residential land use there is a tendency toward neglect and over-occupancy of the residential premises and structures causing substandard housing conditions.

NEXT STEPS

Now that the housing facts are available and the extent of the problem known they must be used in the planning and execution of the program.

A description of the Rehabilitation Program and how it is to be advanced is set forth in the pamphlet "A Plan to Improve Neighborhoods". The plan consists basically of these essential steps:

"1. Field study of housing and neighborhood conditions to obtain the detailed information necessary to determine just what neighborhoods are suitable for this plan and can benefit most from rehabilitation.
2. Selection of neighborhoods on the basis of data obtained in the field study.
3. Once a neighborhood is selected a plan for its improvement will be drawn up and submitted to residents and property owners for suggestions and comment. The plan will then be redrawn and modified to meet the needs of the neighborhood and the desires of its residents.
4. Through community organization, all other ways, even individual contacts, to acquaint all owners and occupants of the neighborhood with the improvement plan and secure action on their part.
5. Secure action by such official agencies as will need to participate. (streets, playgrounds, schools, etc.)
6. Through enforcement, apply the Minimum Housing Standards Ordinance to bring about the needed cleanup, repair and renovation of buildings by those individuals who have not done this voluntarily."

However, if the plan is to be successful in maintaining the ultimate goal of conservation of these neighborhoods, there must be provision for periodic investigations in the rehabilitated areas to see that the improvements are maintained.

The first step in the program has been completed and areas are being selected on the basis of the survey data. The other steps should follow as rapidly as possible. The project has published a Housing Code containing the city laws pertaining to occupied housing with the hope that those interested and concerned will avail themselves of the opportunity of using it as a guide in determining their responsibilities under the <u>Rehabilitation Program</u>. An educational campaign will be launched particularly in the selected areas to acquaint the public with the aims and procedures of this neighborhood conservation program.

The Rehabilitation Program is not a flashy, overnight improvement program and to accomplish visible results will take time, money, initiative, and cooperation of many groups and individuals, but the accomplishments will be of tremendous value to the entire city in the end. The sooner we can start conserving our neighborhoods the more we will save in economic, as well as, human values.

* * *

REBUILDING INDUSTRY - COMMERCE IN ST. LOUIS, 1953

In this proposal for the redevelopment of the financial resources of St. Louis through improvement of its industry and commerce the City Plan Commission made recommendations for local action through rezoning of property for industrial use. In addition, private firms were to be encouraged to cooperate with the city in establishment of parking facilities while the municipality constructed sufficient roadways. The state offered tax relief for improvement of areas. Finally, the commission indicated that Title I of the 1949 Federal Housing Act provided government subsidies for removal of useless buildings and preparation of the land as well as for public housing. All these aids used in a proper fashion would certainly better the city.

(Source: St. Louis City Plan Commission. Rebuilding Industry - Commerce in St. Louis. St. Louis, Missouri, 1953.)

* * *

What Can be done?

. . .at the local level:

Private interests and the City of St. Louis can work together with tools presently available to clear slum areas and make room for industrial and commercial expansion. Authorization for large cities to exercise the right of eminent domain in slum clearance and redevelopment work was granted by the "Urban Redevelopment Corporation Act" of the Missouri Legislature in 1946. The City can, therefore, assist in the assembly of tracts large enough to accomodate new modern industrial and commercial establishment, and can help firms now located in St. Louis to expand their sites. For a tract of 15 or more acres, the Community Unit Plan of the City's zoning ordinance can be used to secure permission for industrial or commercial construction by application to the Board of Public Service, regardless of the zoning district in which the tract is located. The City can also help industry and commerce by carrying out present plans for an express highway system and generally improving its traffic, transit and parking situation for their employees and customers, and possibly by staggering employees' working hours to minimize the peak loads on streets and mass transit facilities.

. . .with the aid of the State

Besides providing the state of eminent domain, the State "Urban Redevelopment Corporation Act" of 1946 provides for significant tax concessions to corporations organized under the law. Any interested group of businesses or individuals could organize a corporation. With taxes presently representing a major burden to industry and commerce, this tax relief provision should prove very attractive to firms which are considering expansion or relocations of their plants.

. . .with Federal aid.

Title I of the Federal "Housing Act" of 1949 provided for slum clearance and redevelopment with subsidation by the Federal government of the cost of removal of obsolete structures and preparation of the land. This law provides for acquisition of land by private interests at a price which is "reasonable" in view of its proposed future use. A "Land Clearance for Redevelopment Authority" was established by the City of St. Louis in February, 1952, to handle the acquisition, preparation and resale of property under Title I. The excess of the cost of purchasing the property and preparing it for use over the "reasonable" resale price is absorbed by the Federal government and the City. In order for an industrial or commercial project to qualify for this Federal aid, it must be designed to redevelop a "predominantly residential" slum area. The problem of permanently relocating residents in another neighborhood will not be too serious, as a large number of new low-rent Public Housing units will soon be made available for low income families in St. Louis.

* * *

DOWNTOWN RENEWAL PLAN, 1960

After a great deal of study and various smaller projects, the city government decided to coordinate all its efforts in order to develop a massive reconstruction program for the downtown and metropolitan area in conjunction with the building of the Jefferson National Expansion Memorial and the celebration of the two hundreth anniversary of the establishment of St. Louis. This plan included dwellings, as well as commercial and industrial buildings, redevelopment of the river front, construction of parkways, and the improvement and increase of mass transit facilities.

(Source: St. Louis. City Plan Commission. <u>A Plan for Downtown St. Louis</u>. St. Louis, 1960.)

The future of Downtown St. Louis is important to the entire metropolitan area.

Downtown St. Louis is the principal retail, wholesale, finance, business and professional center for a metropolitan area of more than 2,000,000 persons. It provides entertainment and cultural activities for the region. It is the center of a large marketing and trading area covering many states.

It is the largest single source of tax revenue for the City, providing almost 20% of all property and other business tax revenues.

More than 100,000 persons are employed downtown.

Downtown houses the major department stores, investment houses, banks, and offices. It has by far the greatest concentration of business space in the netropolitan area.

Governmental offices are concentrated here.

Major sporting events, including college and professional basketball, are regularly featured at Kiel Auditorium, and professional baseball and football are in prospect.

Downtown, already the terminal point of most vehicular traffic in the metropolitan area, will become more important as expressway construction proceeds and these routes converge on the core. It is the principal terminal for buses, and Union Station makes it equally a rail center, and it also provides the main origin and terminus for air passengers.

Thousands of visitors now attend conventions and cultural events each year; as the Jefferson National Expansion Memorial is completed, an additional two million persons will be attracted.

Completion of the Plaza Square Apartments will foster renewed residential living downtown.

Fortunately, downtown has remained quite stable and compact through the years. The center of highest economic value in the city has moved only seven blocks from the river bank where the city was laid out almost 200 years ago. This provides a well-defined area in which to plan.

This report proposes a program of action to make the most of the tremendous investments and existing assets in downtown.

This report is designed to provide a framework within which public and private development can create a workable and exciting center designed for people.

To best serve the region, an easily-accessible, efficient, prosperous, and attractive downtown is needed. The plan points the way to achieve that goal.

METROPOLITAN AREA

Downtown St. Louis has always been the center of a large trade area, the nucleus of a vast transportation network and the heart of the financial and commerical operations of much of mid-America.

The core area occupies less than three-tenths of one percent of the City's area, but it provides employment for nearly one person in four employed in the City.

Historically, St. Louis services a region which extended far to the west and southwest. However, this dominant position has changed because:

1. New centers of commerce and industry have developed in recent decades;
2. Wholesaling and manufacturing methods have changed.

The future character of the central business district will reflect the increasing economic diversification of the region.

The movement of the national center of population toward St. Louis, now only a few miles to the east, provides additional impetus for the growth and expansion of downtown oriented functions.

As the regional core, St. Louis provides the basic facilities for trade and distribution of goods and services; at the same time, the central city absorbs the raw materials and processed goods from the region. Downtown serves as the heart of this interchange.

The Metropolitan St. Louis Area covers parts of five counties and two states. Like its sister cities throughout the country it suffers from congestion, sprawl, blighted areas, population shifts, multiplicity of taxing units and ever-increasing demands for new services.

On the asset side, the St. Louis Metropolitan Area has a highly diversified industrial base; a large skilled labor supply; excellent transportation facilities by rail, road, water and air; abundant water; a strategic national location; ample natural resources nearby and the economic and human capacity to solve its problems.

The heart of this area is the central business district.

In recent years the rapid growth of St. Louis county has appeared to negate the dominant pull of the central core. Congested streets and increased travel time have also lessened its attraction.

Yet the central business district still contains ten percent of the total assessed value of real property in the City, makes a fourth of the City's total retail sales, and provides jobs for 13.5% of all workers in the Metropolitan Area. In addition, the central city offers entertainment and cultural activities as well as facilities for advanced education and training.

With the construction of expressways -- Mark Twain, Ozark, Daniel Boone, and Interstate #44 -- the central business district will again become the single most accessible spot in the area. New highways in Illinois and additional bridges will strengthen the heart of the area -- Downtown St. Louis.

CENTRAL DISTRICT

The central business district for the St. Louis Metropolitan Area -- the shopping, business and financial center, the hard core that we generally call "Downtown St. Louis" -- has been a relatively stable configuration of buildings, streets and transportation terminals. On its periphery are the governmental, civic, industrial and supporting service areas which round out the area under study.

It is a highly concentrated area of people and activities. People on foot, in cars, in buses, the distribution of goods, and service vehicles result in conflicting movements, inconvenience, lost time, and higher operating costs. Concentration has brought congestion which in turn has tended to destroy the concentration which creates it.

In recent years downtown has been affected by moves to non-central locations; its percentage of total retail sales has declined; real estate values have stagnated; access has become difficult, and blighted and slum areas surround it.

What qualities are needed in the central area?

<u>Compactness</u> -- The relatively high density and small area of downtown must be maintained to provide the most efficient interchange of services and materials.

<u>Accessibility</u> -- Projected interstate and urban highways in various stages of completion, will reduce travel time to downtown.

<u>Expressway loop</u> -- A proposed expressway loop around downtown will provide quick and easy access to any portion of the central core. Through traffic will move around the core; local streets will be free for service and access.

<u>Local Circulation</u> -- Additional one-way streets on three sides of the core and streets oriented for efficient utilization of highway ramps will reduce congestion and speed traffic in the central business district.

<u>Parking</u> -- Facilities should be provided in close proximity to highways, with some ramps directly into garages. Short-term spaces can be provided in garages closer to major traffic generators.

<u>Transit</u> -- Mass movement of people via transit is essential to the growth of downtown. A rapid transit system must be developed from the framework offered in the recent transportation study.

<u>Terminal</u> -- A bus terminal should be developed where local and interstate carriers can effect the interchange of passengers economically and conveniently.

<u>Separation of pedestrians and vehicles</u> -- To alleviate hazards, inconveniences and congestion, some separation of these conflicting move-

ments must be ultimately incorporated.

Pedestrian malls -- After the above factors have been implemented, pedestrian malls will be a natural adjunct. Landscaped areas and new vistas will make downtown attractive to its habitants -- businessmen, workers, shoppers, and visitors.

Central Parkway -- The extension of the Memorial Plaza to the east will encourage new development and provide a link between the Jefferson National Expansion Memorial and the Civic Center.

Redevelopment -- Older, blighted areas, such as those in which reconstruction is already contemplated, will instill new vigor into the core values.

Rehabilitation -- Many existing structures must be modernized if the central business district is to meet the challenge that the future offers.

Civic Design -- New and rehabilitated structures and open spaces must be of the highest aesthetic quality to set the tone for total civic design.

These are the steps by which our downtown will respond to the opportunities of the coming decades as an additional million people seek the financial, business and commercial services which only the central business district can offer.

PLANNING AREAS

Downtown has been divided into four planning areas to consider more exactly and conveniently the land uses and remedial treatment required.

1. CORE

The core of the central business district contains the major traffic generating retail facilities, banks and hotels as well as many of the important office buildings. It is the site of the high value corner and the greatest densities of pedestrian movement. Though there is obviously overlap with the other areas, the core area most nearly represents the concept of "Downtown." Basically, the treatment required is continued conservation and rehabilitation. Some few structures will have to be replaced. The immediate goal of any plan must be the preservation of this core area.

2. RIVERFRONT

The area lying east of Broadway between Washington and Poplar contains several office structures which function with the core. Completion of the Jefferson National Expansion Memorial, and the Ozark and Mark Twain Highways, however, will remove most of this area from its position on the periphery of the core and will give it a new function as the "front door" to St. Louis.

Most of this area has now been declared "blighted" under Missouri law and redevelopment treatment seems assured. A carefully designed relationship must be established to link the core and the Jefferson National Expansion Memorial.

3. PARKWAY -- STADIUM

South of the core between Broadway and 12th Street are miscellaneous service functions, warehouses, parking lots, and substandard residences. Much of the area has been declared blighted under the Missouri statute noted above.

A Parkway between Market and Chestnut connecting the Jefferson National Expansion Memorial and the Memorial Plaza is recommended here. This can generate much new development. Redevelopment proposals for a new stadium and supporting facilities have already been projected in this area. Parking garages tied directly to the Daniel Boone expressway will provide further stimulus to redevelopment.

4. PLAZA

Reconstruction in this area to the west of the core is already well underway. The new Federal Building, the Plaza Square Apartments and connecting of Aloe and Memorial Plazas are indicative of the pattern emerging here. Rehabilitation of municipal buildings and a new library annex at 17th and Locust add to the improvements bolstering this portion of the central district.

SUMMARY

The range of activities outlined in this plan represents a dramatic, yet workable and economically feasible approach to the renewal and revitalization of Downtown St. Louis. It establishes the basic framework for traffic and land use, even though additional detailed planning will be required on such items as mass transit, design of open space and service.

Some elements of the plan can be started immediately. Others, such as pedestrian malls, depend upon progress of the expressway, transit program and additional parking garages.

No timetable for completion of the plan has been set forth; the plan is open-ended; more developments will follow as these are completed. . . .

Downtown will be accessible. It can remain compact and efficient. It must be made inviting and attractive. Private and public efforts can achieve these goals. The Plan is a beginning.

ST. LOUIS -- PRESENT AND FUTURE, MAY 7, 1961

These articles are taken from a special section of the St. Louis Post-Dispatch celebrating the enormous strides that had been made in reconstructing the downtown area of St. Louis. The pride taken in the Plaza area as well as in the Riverfront Memorial is evidence of municipal determination to rejeuvenate the city. Preparations were being made for the bicentennial celebration of the founding of St. Louis. In addition, a description is presented of the Missouri-Illinois Bi-State project for industrial development of the St. Louis area.

(Source: St. Louis Post-Dispatch. "Special Progress Section; St. Louis, Today and Tomorrow." St. Louis, May 7, 1961.)

"Plaza Area Transformed"

Urban redevelopment is giving St. Louis a new look and a new outlook. Project Number 1 has created eight and one-half blocks on the edge of the downtown business district and rejeuvenated the Capital Plaza area with 1090 apartments. Project No. 2 now entering the construction phase, will redevelop 100 blocks in Mill Creek Valley with new housing, industrial plants, commercial establishments and buildings for institutions. Project No. 3 is clearing parts of the 71-block Kosciusko area for industry and commerce.

Teamwork between government and private enterprise makes such projects possible. Using federal loans, the city's Land Clearance Authority buys property in blighted areas, tears down the old buildings and sells the cleared ground at reduced price to private interests who agree to redevelop the area in accordance with a prescribed plan that will benefit the community.

The Federal Government defrays two-thirds of the loss incurred in the so-called write down or sale at reduced price, and the city bears the remaining third. Missouri Law offers tax benefits to encourage slum clearance. If a redeveloper agrees to limit annual profits to 8 per cent of project cost, he is taxed for the first 10 years only on the valuation that was placed on the land in its blighted state; for the next 15 years, normal taxes on land and improvements are cut in half.

The Urban Redevelopment Corp. of St. Louis has put up six 13-story apartment buildings in the Plaza area, and will build a group of stores to serve the apartment tenants there. Group Hospital Service is coming into the redevelopment area with a $2,000,000 six-story building to provide offices for the Blue Cross Plan of Hospitalization Insurance. All this involves an investment of more than $18,000,000.

The Plaza Project write down is $2,760,000. Federal grants cover $1,840,000 of this loss. The city has exceeded its required contribution of $920,000 by developing a public park alongside the apartments and making site improvements valued at $1,126,000, so it gets a credit of $206,000 to be applied to the next project.

Clearing 465 acres in Mill Creek and relocating 11,000 persons is the biggest job of urban redevelopment ever undertaken in the United States. It will produce 160 acres of new industrial sites, 25 acres for commercial expansion and 75 acres for erection of 2100 dwelling units in landscaped grounds. St. Louis Redevelopment Corp., organized by local real estate men, will handle all of the industrial, most of the commercial and one-fifth of the residential development. . . .

Federal grants of $11,252,518 have been earmarked to cover two-thirds of the cost of clearing and selling tracts in the Kosciusko area. This project, including development of a South Broadway shopping center and rehabilitation of many old buildings, means investment of over $30,000,000 of private funds.

"Riverfront Memorial To Become a Reality Within Three Years"

The Long, Long Trail leading to development of the Jefferson National Expansion Memorial on the St. Louis riverfront is nearing its end. Civic leaders spent twenty-five years formulating plans, lining up federal aid, then struggling through delays caused by red tape, litigation, the advent of World War II and postwar budgetary troubles, work on the project finally began in 1959, and now is proceeding apace.

The National Park Service says there is every reason to believe that salient features of the Memorial will be created in time for the St. Louis Bicentennial Celebration in 1964. This means that the unsightly railroad trestle on the levee will be done and trains will be moving through the new tunnel; the towering arch conceived by Architect Eero Saarinen will be erected; the underground visitor center at its base and a grand staircase leading down to the levee will be completed, and much of the landscaping will be done.

The memorial will commemorate the Louisiana Purchase, the Lewis and Clarke Expedition and the epoch surge of the American people across rivers, plains, and mountains to the Pacific. . . .

The memorial, to draw perhaps three million visitors a year, will cost about $30,000,000. St. Louis passed a $7,500,000 bond issue to cover its contribution which is being made at the rate of $1 for every $3 of federal outlay. The Terminal Railroad Association contributed $500,000 to help pay for the relocation of the tracks skirting the memorial.

"Making Room for Industrial Growth Plans Call for Big Park at Columbia Bottoms and New Port on Chain of Rocks Canal"

Industrial development in St. Louis area has been hampered by an acute shortage of plant sites on navigable water. Projects to correct this are being pushed on both sides of the Mississippi River.

The Chamber of Commerce of Metropolitan St. Louis proposes to develop a 3,000-acre industrial park at Columbia Bottoms, to form a land tract at the confluence of the Mississippi and the Missouri. This would be a $26,000,000 project financed by tax-free bonds of the Missouri-Illinois Bi-State Development Agency.

Flood protection for Columbia Bottoms will require a $5,000,000 levee. If financing can be worked out by Bi-State, start of construction will be the signal of a drive to sign up buyers of plant sites. Sponsors hope this can be undertaken next fall, with the industrial park to open possible in 1963. . . .

A fund of nearly $330,000 to finance preliminary work on the project has been subscribed by 80 firms in the St. Louis area. . . . The Missouri Highway Department has begun construction of the circumferential expressway which will pass just south of the industrial park site, and have agreed to build the connecting road.

* * *

The port will feature new machinery for high-speed movement of cargo between rail, truck and water carriers. . . .

Emphasis will be placed on handling of raw bulk cargoes -- grain, coal, agricultural fertilizer, steel pipes and wood products and liquid products such as petroleum and crude oils -- rather than manufactured and finished products.

BIBLIOGRAPHY

The works cited have been carefully selected to indicate the major sources to be consulted for further research on the growth and development of St. Louis. Materials listed have been published during the nineteenth and twentieth centuries. The variety of works was chosen to provide a cross-section of the information on the social, economic and political life of the city. Students should also consult the Reader's Guide to Periodical Literature and Social Science and Humanities Index for further articles on St. Louis.

PRIMARY SOURCES

An Act (of Missouri) to revise the Charter of the City of St. Louis and to Extend the Limits Thereof. Approved March 4, 1870. St. Louis, 1870.

Amended City Charter, Approved March 3d, 1851. An Act to Reduce the Law Incorporating the City of St. Louis, and the Several Acts thereof into one Act, and to Amend the Same. St. Louis, 1851.

Charter of the City of St. Louis, Missouri, Adopted by Vote of the People, June 30, 1914. St. Louis, 1914.

Charter of the City of St. Louis, With the Scheme of Separation Between the County of St. Louis and City of St. Louis and Provisions of the Constitution of Missouri Especially Applicable to the City of St. Louis. St. Louis, 1915.

The City Journal; Official Publication of the City of St. Louis, vol. 1, 1920-21-Present.

Civic League of St. Louis. Civic Bulletin. vols. 1 2, 1910-1912. Last issued December, 1912. Replaced by Public Affairs.

------------------------. What the League Is. (What the League Has Done, Officers. . . .) St. Louis, 1909.

Digest of the Charter and the Revised Ordinances of the City of St. Louis, Together with the Constitution of the United States and that of the State of Missouri, and the Several Acts of the General Assembly Relating to the City. St. Louis, 1866.

Governmental Research Institute, St. Louis. The Cost of Registrations and Elections in St. Louis, 1923-34. St. Louis, January, 1935.

--. The Municipal Airport Problem in St. Louis; A Report to Mayor A. P. Kaufmann. St. Louis, 1947.

----------. The St. Louis Police Survey. St. Louis, 1942.

Index St. Louis City Ordinances From Incorporation in 1822 to 1903. ...St. Louis, 1904.

Metropolitan St. Louis Survey. Background for Action. University City, Missouri.

----------. Path of Progress for Metropolitan St. Louis. University City, Missouri, 1957.

Moore, Robert. Vital Statistics of St. Louis Since 1840. St. Louis, 1904.

Nasatir, Abraham P., ed. Before Lewis and Clark; Documents Illustrating the History of Missouri, 1785-1804. St. Louis, 1952.

The Ordinance of the City of St. Louis, State of Missouri, Digested and Revised by the Common Council of Said City in the Year 1860 and 1861, with...the Various Charters of the City of St. Louis. St. Louis, 1871.

An Ordinance to Prevent Ill Feeling, Conflict, and Collisions Between the White and Colored Races in the City of St. Louis, and to Preserve the Public Peace and Promote the General Welfare by Making Reasonable Provisions Requiring the Use of Separate Blocks for Residence by White and Colored People Respectively. St. Louis, 1916.

The Ordinances of the City of St. Louis, State of Missouri, Digested and Revised by the City Council of Said City, in the Years 1855-6 with...the Various Charters of the City of St. Louis. St. Louis, 1856.

Public Affairs. A Monthly Record of Civic and Social Progress in St. Louis. vol. 1-2, 1913-1914. Ceased publication 1914.

The Revised Code of St. Louis (general ordinances). Being Revising Ordinance Number 22902, Approved March 19, 1907. ...St. Louis, 1907.

The Revised Code of St. Louis, 1912. ...St. Louis, 1913.

The Revised Code of St. Louis, 1914. (general Ordinances), Being Revising Ordinance No. 20,013, Approved April 12, 1918; Supplemented by an Appendix Containing the General Ordinances Enacted between February 14, 1918; and the Summer, 1918. ...

with...the Charter of the City of St. Louis; a Compilation of State Laws especially applicable to the City of St. Louis;... St. Louis, 1918.

The Revised Code of St. Louis, 1926 (general ordinances) Being Revising Ordinance Number 36,614, Approved March 7, 1928;... St. Louis, 1928.

The Revised Code of the City of St. Louis, Missouri, 1960. St. Louis, 1961-.

The Revised Ordinance of the City of St. Louis, 1887 To Which Are Prefixed...the Scheme for the Separation of the Governments of the City and County of St. Louis and the Charter of the City. St. Louis, 1887.

The Revised Ordinance, City of St. Louis, No. 17188. Approved April 7, 1893...St. Louis, 1895.

The Revised Ordinance of the City of St. Louis Together with...the Scheme for the Separation of the Governments of the City and County of St. Louis, the Charter of the City, and a Digest of the Laws Applicable to the City. St. Louis, 1881.

The Revised Ordinances of the City of St. Louis, Revised and Digested by the City Council, in the Year 1850, with...the Various Charters of, and Laws Applicable to the Town and City of St. Louis. St. Louis, 1850.

St. Louis Chamber of Commerce. St. Louis As It Is Today. Issued by the St. Louis Chamber of Commerce and "Visit St. Louis" Committee. St. Louis, 1951.

St. Louis Chamber of Commerce, Charities Committee. Charitable and Philanthropic Organizations of St. Louis. 1920-date.

St. Louis Citizens' Committee. Report of the Engineer Board to the Citizens' Committee on Lowering Tracks of the Missouri Pacific Railroad, and Connecting all Commercial Outlets of St. Louis. June 1, 1874. St. Louis, 1874.

St. Louis City Plan Commission. Annual Report. St. Louis, 1917-1947. Ceased publication with 1946-/47.

----------------------------. Comprehensive City Plan. St. Louis, 1947.

----------------------------. Comprehensive Plan, Saint Louis. 2 parts. St. Louis, 1948-(49).

----------------------------. The Housing Problem in St. Louis. St.

Louis, 1920.

——————————————. The Kingshighway. A Report by the City Plan Commission, January 23, 1917. St. Louis, 1917. Description of highway and improvements to be made when it is completed.

——————————————. Let's Look at Housing; A Report on Housing Conditions in Selected Areas of St. Louis. St. Louis, 1953.

——————————————. Measuring Deterioration in Commercial and Industrial Areas: The Development of a Method. A Demonstration Project. St. Louis, 1957.

——————————————. A Plan for the Central River Front, Saint Louis, Missouri. St. Louis, 1928.

——————————————. Plan for Downtown St. Louis. St. Louis, 1960.

——————————————. Plan for Public Recreational Areas. St. Louis, 1944.

——————————————. Rebuilding Industry -- Commerce in Saint Louis. St. Louis, 1953.

——————————————. Recreation in St. Louis. St. Louis, 1917.

——————————————. St. Louis After the War. St. Louis, 1918.

——————————————. Saint Louis After World War II. St. Louis, 1942.

——————————————. The St. Louis Transit System, Present and Future. St. Louis, 1920.

St. Louis Comptroller's Office. Report for the Fiscal Year. 1875/76-date. St. Louis, 1877-date.

——————————————. Synopsis of Expenditures of the City. . . for the Fiscal Year 1905/06-date. St. Louis, 1907-date.

St. Louis Council. Journal. 1874/75 - 1912/13. St. Louis, 1875-1913. Ceased Publication, 1913.

St. Louis Delegates to the Chicago River and Harbor Convention, 1847. The Commerce and Navigation of the Valley of the Mississippi, and also that Appertaining to the City of St. Louis: Considered, with Reference to the Improvement by the General Government of the Mississippi River and Its Principal Tributaries. . . .St. Louis, 1897.

BIBLIOGRAPHY

St. Louis Department of Public Welfare. Division of Parks and Recreation. Annual Report. 1894/95-date. St. Louis, 1895-date.

St. Louis Education Board. Annual Report. 1853/54-date. St. Louis, 1854-date.

St. Louis Health Department. Annual Report of the Commissioner. 1877/78-date. St. Louis, 1879-date.

──────────────────────. Bulletin. vol. 1-23. July, 1912-April, 1933. St. Louis, 1912-33. Ceased publication in 1933.

──────────────────────. . . .Vital Statistics. May, 1899-March, 1910: Statement of Mortality, Vital Statistics. . .and Local Meteorology.

──────────────────────. Statement of Vital Statistics. . .St. Louis, April, 1910-1923.

──────────────────────. Statistical Reports. St. Louis, 1934-date.

──────────────────────. Vital Statistics. St. Louis, 1924-33.

St. Louis House of Delegates. Journal. 1877/78-1913/14. St. Louis, 1878-1914. Ceased Publication with 1913/14.

St. Louis Louisiana Purchase Exposition. 1904. The Greatest of Expositions, Completely Illustrated; Official Publication. St. Louis, 1904.

St. Louis Mayor's Transit Ownership Committee. Majority Report. St. Louis, 1952.

──. Report. St. Louis, 1952.

St. Louis Mercantile Library Association. Constitution and By-Laws. Originally adopted 1846. As Revised January, 1896. St. Louis, 1896.

St. Louis Police Department. Allocation of Patrol Man Power Resources in the Saint Louis Police Department; An Experiment. 2 vols. St. Louis, 1966.

──────────────────────. Police Journal. vol. 1-22. 1912/13-1933. Suspended publication May 20, 1933.

St. Louis Post-Dispatch. 50th Anniversary Number. St. Louis, 1928.

──────────────────────. "St. Louis Bicentennial, 1764-1964; an Era of Greatness." St. Louis, 1964.

──────────────────────. "Special Progress Section; St. Louis, Today and Tomorrow." St. Louis, 1961.

St. Louis Public Library. Annual Report. 1865/70-date. St. Louis, 1865-date.

----------------------. Monthly Bulletin. 1879-1939. St. Louis, 1879-1939. Ceased publication February, 1939. The title from 1879 to 1883 was St. Louis Public School Library Bulletin.

----------------------. St. Louis Public Library Magazine. St. Louis, April, 1897-November, 1898.

St. Louis Public Safety Department. . . .Report and Recommendations. 1937/38-date. St. Louis, 1938-date.

St. Louis Public Safety Department. Fire and Prevention Division. Annual Report. : .1909/10-1937/38. St. Louis, 1910-1938. Beginning 1938/39 it was included in the Report and Recommendations of the Public Safety Department.

St. Louis Public Schools Board. Annual Report of the General Superintendent of the. . .Public Schools. vols. 1-42, 1854-1895/96. Continued under St. Louis Public Education Board.

St. Louis Public Utilities Department. Annual Report, 1936/37-date. St. Louis, 1937-date.

St. Louis Register's Office. Annual Report of the City Register for the Fiscal Year 1892/93-1915/16. Ceased publication with 1915/16.

St. Louis Sewer Department. Annual Report of the Sewer Commissioner. 1889/90-1913/14. See St. Louis Missouri Streets and Sewers Departments for publications after August 28, 1914.

St. Louis Stock Exchange. Constitution and By-Laws of the "St. Louis Stock-Exchange." St. Louis, 1903.

St. Louis Streets and Sewers Department. Annual Report. 1914/15-Date. St. Louis, 1915-date. From 1933 to 34 and from 1939 to 40 the title was What the Taxpayer Gets for His Money. Annual Report.

St. Louis Water Commissioner. Annual Report. 1865-date. St. Louis, 1865-date.

The Scheme for the Government of the County and City of St. Louis and Charter for the City of St. Louis, as Proposed by the Board of Freeholders, Acting Under and in Pursuance of Section 20, Article IX of the Constitution of the State of Missouri. St. Louis, 1876.

SECONDARY SOURCES

Alvord, Idress. Historical and Interesting Places of St. Louis. St. Louis,

BIBLIOGRAPHY   145

1909.

Anderson, Galusha. The Story of a Border City During the Civil War. Boston, 1908. This is a sketch of local conditions and feelings as revealed through observations and experiences. It shows the problems involved in the struggle between opposing factions.

Beckwith, Paul E. Creoles of St. Louis. St. Louis, 1893.

Berthold, Eugenie. Glimpses of Creole Life in Old St. Louis. St. Louis, 1933.

Billon, Frederic L. Annals of St. Louis in Its Early Days Under the French Spanish Dominations. St. Louis, 1886. This is a good source for the early history of the area.

Bollens, John C. Exploring the Metropolitan Community. Berkeley, California, 1961. This is a valuable study of the problems of the city and its surrounding territory.

The Book of St. Louisans; A Biographical Dictionary of Leading Living Men of the City of St. Louis and Vicinity. St. Louis, 1912.

Booker T. Washington Trading Stamp Association, St. Louis. Metropolitan St. Louis Negro Directory; A Classified Publication of Biographies, Business, Professional, Religious, Social, Fraternal, Welfare, Industrial and Labor Organizations. St. Louis, 1945.

Boyer, Mary J. The Old Gravois Coal Diggings. Festus, Missouri, 1954. This work presents some necessary information concerning the early days of St. Louis and the surrounding area.

Burke, Harry R. From the Day's Journey; A Book of By-paths and Eddies about Saint Louis. St. Louis, 1924.

Carson, William G.B. Managers in Distress; the St. Louis Stage, 1840-1844. St. Louis, 1949. Important study about cultural life during this period is presented.

Compton, Charles H. Fifty Years of Progress of the St. Louis Public Library, 1876-1926. St. Louis, 1926.

Cox, James. Old and New St. Louis. A Concise History of the Metropolis of the West. With a Biographical Appendix Compiled by the Central Biographical Publishing Company. St. Louis, 1894.

Coyle, Elinor M. Saint Louis; Portrait of a River City. St. Louis, 1966. This is an interesting historical and descriptive sketch of the City.

Darby, John F. Personal Recollections of Many Prominent People Whom

I Have Known, and of Events -- Especially of Those Relating to the History of St. Louis -- During the First Half of the Present Century. St. Louis, 1880.

Edwards, Richard and M. Hopewell. Edwards' Great West and Her Commerical Metropolis, Embracing a General View of the West and a Complete History of St. Louis. . . .St. Louis, 1860. This is an interesting analysis of the West, the history of St. Louis and its press up to the mid-nineteenth century.

Fanning, William H. W. Historical Sketch of the St. Louis University. St. Louis, 1908.

Gill, McCune. The St. Louis Story; Library of American Lives, 1952. A Source Edition Recording the Early and Contemporary History of St. Louis City and County. . . .3 vols. Hopkinsville, Kentucky, 1952. This is an interesting and important source for the study of St. Louis history.

Gray, Kenneth E. A Report on Politics in Saint Louis. Cambridge, Massachusetts, 1961. This is a good study of politics.

Hanson, John W. The Official History of the Fair, St. Louis, 1904. . . . St. Louis, 1904. This is an important book because of the historical importance of the celebration of the Louisiana Purchase.

Hart, Jim A. A History of the St. Louis Globe-Democrat. Columbia, Missouri, 1961. This is an interesting study of the paper and press in St. Louis.

Hill, Walter H. Historical Sketch of the St. Louis University; the Celebration of its 50th Anniversary or Golden Jubilee, on June 24, 1879. St. Louis, 1879.

Holderness, Marvin E. Curtain Time in Forest Park; A Narrative of the St. Louis Municipal Opera, 1919-1958. St. Louis, 1960. This is a valuable account of this very interesting and unusual opera company in the United States.

Hyde, William and H. L. Conrad, eds. Encyclopedia of the History of St. Louis. . .New York, 1899.

Kennerly, William Clark. Persimmon Hill, A Narrative of Old St. Louis and the Far West. (As told to Elizabeth Russell) Norman, Oklahoma, 1948. These are family reminiscences arranged by the daughter of the author from his papers which present a picture of the development of St. Louis and the West.

Kirschten, Ernest. Catfish and Crystal. Garden City, New York, 1960. This newspaperman presents a picture of St. Louis from its beginnings under the French up to the present. He describes many people and events of national and local significance.

Lange, Dena and Merlin Ames. St. Louis; Child of the River-Parent of the West. St. Louis, 1939. This is an interesting sketch and description of the city.

Lionberger, Isaac H. The Annals of St. Louis, and a Brief Account of Its Foundation and Progress, 1764-1928. St. Louis, 1929. This work is a good historical study of St. Louis and is valuable when used in conjunction with other histories.

MacAdam, David H. Tower Grove Park of the City of St. Louis. Review of Its Origin and History, Plan of Improvement, Ornamental Features,. . .St. Louis, 1883.

McDermott, John F. The Early Histories of St. Louis. St. Louis, 1952.

——————————. The French in the Mississippi Valley. Urbana, Illinois, 1965. The author presents the early history of the city as given in fourteen papers at the conference observing the two hundreth anniversary of the founding of St. Louis.

Musick, James B. St. Louis as a Fortified Town; a Narrative and Critical Essay of the Period of Struggle for the Fur Trade of the Mississippi Valley and its Influence Upon St. Louis. St. Louis, 1941.

Perry, Charles Milton, ed. The St. Louis Movement in Philosophy, Some Source Material. Norman, Oklahoma, 1930. This work presents a bibliography of various members of the movement and some letters pertaining to it.

Peterson, Charles E. Colonial St. Louis; Building a Creole Capital. St. Louis, 1949.

Powell, Lyman P. Historic Towns of the Western States. New York, 1901.

Proetz, Arthur W. I Remember You, St. Louis. St. Louis, 1963. This is a presentation of reminiscences of life in St. Louis.

Rammelkamp, Julian S. Pulitzer's Post-Dispatch, 1878-1883. Princeton, New Jersey, 1967. This study examines the Post-Dispatch during its early years as a basis for Pulitzer's success. St. Louis is shown as one of the two bases of Pulitzer's career.

Rombauer, Robert J. The Union Cause in St. Louis in 1861. An Historical Sketch. St. Louis, 1909.

St. Louis Chamber of Commerce. Metropolitan St. Louis in Missouri.

Jefferson City, Missouri, 1955. This is a good general description of the city along with its parks, businesses and essential services.

St. Louis First National Bank. St. Louis: A Fond Look Back. An Appreciation of Its Community by the First National Bank in St. Louis on the Occasion of the One Hundreth Anniversary of the Founding of Its Predecessors the Southern Bank and the Mechanics Bank in 1856. St. Louis, 1956.

St. Louis Society of Automobile Pioneers. A History of Automobiles in St. Louis and the Part that City Has Taken in the Development of the Automobile. St. Louis, 1930.

Scharf, John Thomas. History of Saint Louis City and County, from the Earliest Periods to the Present Day: Including Biographical Sketches of Representative Men. 2 vols. Philadelphia, 1883.

Seifert, Shirley. The Key to St. Louis. Philadelphia, 1963. This is a short account of the history and development of the city.

Shepard, Elihu H. The Early History of St. Louis and Missouri From Its First Exploration by White Men in 1673 to 1843. St. Louis, 1870.

Snider, Denton Jacques. The St. Louis Movement in Philosophy, Literature, Education, Psychology,. . .St. Louis, 1920. This is an interesting and enlightening work concerning the cultural movement which had its headquarters in St. Louis.

Snow, Marshall S. The City Government of St. Louis. Baltimore, 1887.

Spencer, Thomas E. The Story of Old St. Louis. St. Louis, 1914.

Stevens, Walter Barlow. St. Louis, the Fourth City, 1764-1909. 3 vols. St. Louis, 1909. Presents a detailed account of the history, industry, commerce and businessmen of St. Louis.

Traubel, Helen. St. Louis Woman. (In collaboration with Richard G. Hubler.) New York, 1959. This is the autobiography of the great American singer.

Vogel, Rachel Fram. Social Life in St. Louis (1764-1804). St. Louis, 1921.

Wade, Richard C. The Urban Frontier, Chicago, 1964.

Wells, Rolla. Episodes of My Life. St. Louis, 1933. These are personal experiences of this former mayor of St. Louis.

Wetmore, Claude. The Battle Against Bribery. Being the Narrative of Joseph Folk's Warfare on Boodlers. . .St. Louis, 1904. This is an early account of the war on corruption in St. Louis by the man who was to buck his party and eventually become governor of Missouri.

ARTICLES

Barclay, Thomas S. "The Movement for Municipal Home Rule in St. Louis," University of Missouri Studies, vol. XVIII, 1943, 1-138.

Black, Arline. "Captain James Mackay, Early St. Louis Settler," Missouri Historical Bulletin, vol. XI, January, 1955, 187-190.

Covington, James W. "The Camp Jackson Affair, 1861," Missouri Historical Review, vol. LV, April, 1961, 197-212.

Delassus, Charles D. "Diary of Charles Dehault Delassus from New Orleans to St. Louis, 1836," ed. by John Francis McDermott, Louisiana Historical Quarterly, vol. XXX, 1947, 359-438.

Dodson, G. R. "An Interpretation of the St. Louis Philosophical Movement," Journal of Philosophy and Scientific Methods, vol. VI, 1909, 337-345.

Forbes, Cleon. "The St. Louis School of Thought," Missouri Historical Review, vol. XXV, 1930, 83-101, 289-305, 461-473, 608-622. vol. XXVI, 1931, 68-77.

Garraghan, Gilbert J. "The First Settlement on the Site of St. Louis," Illinois Catholic Historical Review, vol. IX, 1927, 342-347.

Isaacs, Deborah. "Ante Bellum Days in St. Louis," Glimpses of the Past (Missouri Historical Society), vol. V, 141-155.

Lass, William E. "Tourists' Impressions of St. Louis, 1766-1859," Missouri Historical Review, vol. LII, July, 1958, 325-336.

McDermott, John Francis. "The Confines of a Wilderness," Missouri Historical Review, vol. XXIX, 1934, 1-12.

Peterson, Charles E. "Colonial St. Louis," Missouri Historical Society Bulletin, April, 1947, 94-111, and subsequent nos.

Smit, William M. "Old Broadway, A Forgotten Street, and Its Park of Mounds," Missouri Historical Society Bulletin, April, 1948, 153-163.

Stolee, Ingeborg B. "The St. Louis Christmas Carolers," Christmas, 1944, 13-18.

Williams, Helen Devault. "Social Life in St. Louis from 1840 to 1860," Missouri Historical Review, vol. XXXI, 1936, 10-24.

NAME INDEX

Ahe, Chris Von der, 36
Alt, Dr. Adolph, 38
Anheuser, Eberhard, 17
Audubon, John J., 9

Balmer, Charles, 8
Barnes, Robert A., 44
Barnett, Mayor Arthur Buckner, 30
Barry, Mayor James G., 12
Bauer, Professor Louis, 26
Beausoliel, Captain, 1
Becker, Mayor William D., 59
Belgrano, Frank N., Jr., 58
Bell, William, 24
Benton, Thomas Hart, 14
Berry, G. L., 61
Binger, Dr., 19
Blow, Susan E., 29
Boya, Captain Joseph, 49
Britton, Mayor Henry, 30
Brookes, Rev. James H., 22
Brown, Governor B. Gratz, 27
Brown, Mayor Joseph, 27
Bryan, William Jennings, 49
Burr, Aaron, 2
Busch, August A., Jr., 62, 63
Butler, Colonel Edward, 45, 51, 53

Cabot, Frank J., 45
Cairns, Mrs. Anne Sneed, 20
Calvin, James M., 43
Camden, Mayor Peter G., 11
Carmichael, Stokely, 68
Carpenter, Dr. A.N., 44
Carr, William C., 8
Cervantes, Mayor A.J., 66, 68
Chouteau, Auguste, 1
Chouteau, Pierre, 52
Clark, General George Rogers, 1
Clark, Captain William, 3
Clay, Henry, 10
Clemens, Samuel L., [pseud. Mark Twain], 19
Cleveland, President Grover, 40
Cobbs, William, 68
Cole, Mayor Nathan, 27

Compton, W.R., 55
Cox, Pastor A.C., 22
Curtiss, Glen, 54

Daggett, Mayor John D., 8
Danforth, William H., 46
Darby, Mayor John F., 6, 7, 8
Darst, Mayor Joseph H., 61
Dearmont, Russell L., 61
Dickens, Charles, 9
Dickman, Mayor Bernard F., 58, 59
Donovan, Daniel C., 51
Dubourg, Bishop, 4

Edwards, Richard, 19
Eliot, Dr. William G., 9
Eliot, Rev. W.G., 6
Essen, Fred, 55
Ewing, Mayor William L., 36

Fanning, M.A., 43
Farley, James, Postmaster General, 58
Filley, Mayor Chauncey Ives, 22
Filley, Mayor Oliver Dwight, 19
Fitzpatrick, Daniel R., 63
Fletcher, Governor, 23
Flint, Mrs. Leta, 47
Folk, Joel Wingate, 53
Fox, Abraham, 5
Francis, Mayor David R., 38
French, Dr. Pinckney, 44
Frost, Dr. D.M., 52

Garesche, Mrs. Vital M., 9
Gehrum, Jonas, 56
Giddings, Salmon, 3
Gouley, George F., 25

Hannegan, Robert E., Postmaster General, 61
Harnicke, Lieutenant Felix H., 52
Harris, Dr. William Torrey, 18
Harrison, Edward, 51

Harrison, William Henry, Governor, 2
Hawes, Henry, 50
Hayes, R., 67
Hellmich, Arnold J., 56
Helmuth, Dr., 26
Hendricks, Thomas A., 32
Hicks, Rev. John J., 64, 65
Higginbotham, Rev. John, 12
Hobart, Garret A., 49
How, Mayor John, 15, 17
Howard, Benjamin, 2
Hughes, Dr. Charles H., 44

Jackson, President Andrew, 5
Jefferson, President Thomas, 2
John XXIII, Pope, 63
Johnson, President Lyndon B., 65, 66
Johnson, Senator Edwin C., 63
Johnston, Colonel John W., Mayor, 6
Julian, V., 62

Kaufmann, Mayor Aloys P., 59, 60
Keel, Mayor Henry W., 54, 55
Keismann, Mayor Frederick, 54
Kennett, Mayor Luther M., 13
King, Mayor Worthington, 16
King, Mrs. Julia Field, 45
Kinney, Senator Michael J., 56
Koen, Charles, 68
Kram, Mayor John M., 12

Laclede, Pierre, 1
Lane, Dr. William Carr, Mayor, 4, 7
Leffingwell, Hiram, 26
Lewis, Dr. Bransford, 44
Lewis, Captain Merriwether, 2
Lind, Jenny, 14
Lindbergh, Charles, 57
Linton, Dr. M. L., 9
Louis XV, King of France, 1

McCaffrey, president of school board, 64
MacDowell, Dr. Joseph N., 8
McKee, William, 14
McKinley, William, 49
McKinstry, Major, 21
McLure, Mrs. M.A.E., 43
McNari, Alexander, 4
McNeil, Ebenezer, 14
Madison, President James, 2
Maguire, Mayor George, 9
Marshall, Vice President Thomas Riley, 54
Martin, Dr. S.C., 46
Massot, Eugene L., 19
Mayfield, Dr. W.H., 46
Merwin, J.B., 24
Miles, Clarence W., 62
Miller, Mayor Victor J., 56, 57
Miller, William, 6
Mitchell, Tobias, 51
Moore, H.D., 19, 20
Morris, Dr. C.C., 46
Mullanphy, Bryan, 11
Mullanphy, John, 5

Nollau, Rev. L.E., 18
Noonan, Mayor Edward A., 41

O'Fallon, Colonel John, 5, 30
Ohman-Dumesnil, Dr. A., 46
Overstolz, Mayor Henry, 32

Page, Mayor Daniel O., 5
Parks, Oliver L., 60
Peckham, John, 21
Piggott, Captain James, 2
Pike, Zebulon M., 2
Powell, Adam Clayton, Jr., 68
Pratte, Mayor Bernard, 10
Pulitzer, Joseph, 18, 23, 27, 29, 34, 63
Pulitzer, Joseph, Jr., 63

Queeny, John F., 52

Reed, Senator, 55
Rigauche, Madame Marie Payant, 2
Rotchford, Mr., 2
Rozell, Arthur, 50

Saigh, F.M., Jr., 61, 62
Schurz, Carl, 18
Sever, Henry E., 59
Sewall, Arthur, 49
Seymour, Thomas W., 49
Shaw, Henry, 25
Simpson, Delos A., 33, 41
Singer, Bernard, 34
Smith, Governor, 61, 62
Smith, Samuel D., 15
Steinberger, Leonard, 27
Stephens, Governor Lon, 50
Stovall, Chester E., 65
Swope, Gerard, 56

Taylor, Mayor Daniel Gilchrist, 20
Thomas, Mayor James S., 22
Thorpe, Dr. T.J., 49
Thurman, Allen G., 40
Tilden, Samuel J., 32
Trudeau, Jean Baptiste, 1
Tucker, Mayor Raymond R., 62, 63, 65, 66

Twain, Mark. See Clemens, Samuel L.

Valentine, Dr. Philo G., 33
Veeck, Bill, 62
Vincil, Dr. John D., 43
Voort, Antoni Van der, 59

Walbridge, Mayor Cyrus P., 45
Walker, Jesse, 4
Walrup, Mrs. Helen, 45
Walsh, D., 68
Walsingham, W., 62
Ward, Rev. John, 4
Warner, Mayor Charles G., 49
Watson, James S., 15
Watson, Thomas, 49
Weber, Henry, 8
Wells, Mayor Rolla, 50, 53, 54
Whalen, Michael J., 56
Whelan, Eli M., 13
Wiggin, Mrs. Lucy A., 39
Wilson, John C., 5
Wilson, President Woodrow, 54
Wimer, Mayor John M., 9, 18
Wyman, Edward, 9

Ziegenhein, Mayor Henry, 51